DISCOVERING ANGELS

Theolyn Cortens

CAER SIDI PUBLICATIONS
OXFORDSHIRE
1996

Second edition published 1996
First published in Angeland 1992
CAER SIDI PUBLICATIONS
Hencroft, Main Road
Long Hanborough
Oxfordshire OX8 8LA

Designed by Will Shaman
at The Flying Pyramid Factory Ltd., Oxfordshire

ISBN 1-898632-02-2

Cover printing: Windrush Press, Witney, Oxfordshire
Text printing and binding: Short Run Press Ltd., Exeter

Typeset in 10 on 12pt Monotype Galliard

ABOUT THE AUTHOR

Theolyn Cortens is a mystic and visionary writer who has been exploring deep realms of consciousness in one way or another for most of her life.

She has a degree in Philosophy and Literature and has worked in adult education and as an astrologer. In 1974 she had an extraordinary visitation which led her to investigate the worlds of the Archangels. Her aim is to share the techniques she has developed for reaching into these realms. Her courses and workshops are based around the Timeless Wisdom and draw on the Western Mystical tradition for imagery and insights.

'We each contain, within our consciousness, the vast extent of Creation, the angels and archangels, cherubim and seraphim – as without, so within. The stuff of Creation is very simple, and we are part of it, there is only one Reality and we are in it.'

DEDICATION

This book is dedicated with love and admiration to those intrepid explorers of the interior, Teresa of Avila and William Blake, without whom I would have been lost in the undergrowth.

It is also dedicated to my own children, and grandchildren, and all children everywhere, with the certainty that future generations will be able to walk every moment in Morning Glory.

What is now proved was once only imagined.   — William Blake

...very often the soul is utterly blinded, absorbed, amazed and dazzled by the wonders that it sees.   — Teresa of Avila

ACKNOWLEDGEMENTS

The author wishes to acknowledge permissions from the publishers of the following books:

Kahlil Gibran: *The Prophet*, first published by William Heinemann Ltd. 1926

Roger Cook: *The Tree of Life*, published by Thames and Hudson Ltd. in their Art and Imagination series, copyright Roger Cook 1974

C. T. Onions (ed.), *Shorter Oxford English Dictionary*, copyright Oxford University Press, 1974

Maxine Rodinson: *Mohammed*, trans. Anne Carter (Allen Lane The Penguin Press 1971) Copyright Club Francais du livre 1961, trans. copyright Anne Carter 1971

Melanie Reinhart: *Chiron and the Healing Journey, An astrological and psychological perspective*, published by Arkana, copyright Melanie Reinhart 1989

D.H. Lawrence: *Shadows*, acknowledgments to the literary agents Lawrence Pollinger Ltd. and the Estate of Frieda Lawrence

C. S. Lewis: *The Lion, the Witch and the Wardrobe*, published by Lions, an imprint of Harper Collins Publishers Ltd., copyright the Estate of C.S. Lewis

Richard Wilhelm translation: *I Ching, the Book of Changes*, trans. Cary F. Barnes, Arkana 1989, first published in England by Routledge and Kegan Paul Ltd, copyright Bollingen Foundation Inc. 1950, 1970

Dylan Thomas: *The force that through the green fuse drives the flower* from *The Poems*, published by Dent in the Everyman Series, permission acknowledged from the literary agents, David Higham Associates Ltd.

T. S. Eliot: *Little Gidding* and *East Coker*, published by Faber and Faber

Z'ev ben Shimon Halevi: *Kabbalah*, published by Thames and Hudson in their *Art and Imagination* series, copyright Warren Kenton 1979

Z'ev Ben Shimon Halevi: *The Tree of Life: an introduction to the Kabbalah*, published by Rider, copyright Warren Kenton 1972

Acknowledgments also to Charlotte Macleod for a short extract from her excellent book *Trusting: Astrology for Sceptics*, published by Turnstone Press in 1973 – I have been unable to trace the right people to seek formal permission.

I have not had a reply to my request for permission to quote from:

Ibn'Arabi: *Journey to the Lord of Power*, trans. Rabia Terri Harris, published by East-West Publications (UK) Ltd., 1981

CONTENTS

INTRODUCTION

I first met with an Archangel in the summer of 1974. It was an awe-inspiring experience which still makes me tremble. A couple of days before the event I was given a premonition in the form of the following poem:

Vision

Last night I woke
And saw an Angel
Seated on my bed.

In starched white linen
With alabaster hands
And gleaming feathers
On molten, golden wings.

A face of such stern gentleness
As carved in Florence marble,
Surrounded by a nimbus
Of such light as human eyes
Could not gaze upon
And overwhelmed the mechanics of my brain.

So motionless, so still,
It gazed with eyes
I feared to meet,
For it seemed that
Within their timeless orbs
I might lose all knowledge of myself.

The experience that followed is well described by the poem, although the 'visitor' arrived at mid-day, not in the night. I had been ill and unable to work for several weeks. During this time I had been having extraordinary dreams and found deep, uninterrupted sleep impossible. I had felt threatened by invisible forces and had resorted to repeated patterns of prayer in an attempt to centre myself. During the morning of Sunday 23rd June I felt a distinct alteration in my state of consciousness; I became much more peaceful and experienced a sense of expansion and bliss. At the same time I became aware that something extraordinary was about to happen to me. I consulted with *I Ching* and threw the hexagram 'Inner Truth'. The reading, from Wilhelm's translation, spoke of a 'light-giving power', which must quicken the germ of life with in the egg, 'if life is to be awakened'. My certainty that I was waiting for some kind of unusual event was enhanced by this reading. Just before lunchtime, at approximately one o'clock, I felt the sense of expectation intensifying and I went upstairs to my bedroom. I heard voices inside my head, telling me I was going to meet God, and when I lay down and closed my eyes I was taken over by a brilliant golden light which pulsated throughout my whole being. It is extremely difficult to identify how long the experience lasted – it may have only taken a few seconds, though it felt like several minutes. As the light began to enter my body, starting in the head, I did try to ask, 'Who are you?', but I had no response. The gathering energy of the light overtook me; I do not think I completely lost my awareness of being at any point, although I lost all contact with my surroundings and my sense of being in the world. The energy was demanding and persistent; every cell in my system was illuminated by a light which made sunshine seem like the light produced by a low-watt light bulb. The pulsing light came to a climax and rushed upwards through my body and out through the top of my head, in a burst of brilliant red and a fluttering of white. I came back to myself on the bed and sat up, wondering whether I had met an angel or had suffered some kind of fit.

The images of white linen and alabaster in my precognitive poem are a little cool to represent the power and brilliance of the presence, but it certainly 'overwhelmed the mechanics of my brain', and for several weeks afterwards I had very little 'knowledge of myself'; I was totally invaded by a dynamic, transpersonal energy which shook my body, mind and spirit to its core. I was shown a metaphysical world and given brief insights into the underlying structures of nature. I was in beatific state, a state of innocence and bliss:

Jubilation

This is the flame,
The rose-sweet fire,
That consumes the
Age-old bird in
Its shining byre.

I am turned on
The Creator's wheel,
Centred in a
Silvered goblet,
A shining shield.
I am heralded

By sweet voices, and
Gossamer wings
Attend the haloed
Choir-boy who sings.

I am frozen
And time stands still
In the empty citadel:
No sound…no breath…
Until the first bell
Fragments eternity,
The first prism
Splinters the light,

The egg hatched,
The bird bright,
The first song
In Adam's Eden
And I AM there.

At the time, and for some years afterwards, I assumed that this energy must be Gabriel, since I really didn't know about other Archangels, and the visit seemed to have something in common with Mahomet's description of the Archangel Gabriel. What I did know of Gabriel indicated that it usually arrived with a message and there was no obvious message involved in this visit.

A moment or so before I was overtaken by the extraordinary light and power of the visitation I heard sweet voices telling me to 'Prepare to meet your God'. I really had no choice! It crossed my mind briefly that the phrase might indicate that I was going to die. It was a death of a kind: Mahomet said, 'You must die before you die', meaning that the small self must be totally annihilated, completely surrendered to the transcendent. (Islam means 'surrender' and a Muslim is anyone who surrenders to God). Was the light I encountered, that invaded me, God, rather than any angel, or Archangel? To meet God would mean a total loss of self-consciousness, at least temporarily, and although that may have happened there is no way one would remember it. The invasion, for that's how I felt about it, seemed purposeful, it had a sense of direction, it pulsed through every cell of my physiology. The light started at the top of my head, creeping under my closed eyes like brilliant sunshine does when you lie on a beach. As it filled all the other corners of me it vibrated and reached a climactic peak: it was erotic and reminded me of what little I had read of

Teresa of Avila's angel. Afterwards, when I looked at the question with a scientific eye I thought maybe I had had some kind of fit: when I consulted medical books I couldn't find references to such experiences. Epileptics have auras and precognition but the fit is not experienced; by that time self-consciousness has disappeared. It was a nice idea – after all a grand-mal fit involves a high discharge of electrical energy and part of me was quite prepared to 'explain' the phenomenon in such terms.

One thing I discovered, while hunting for medical explanations, was that the drugs I had been given for asthma can cause too much electrical activity in the brain. I had also had mumps, which can lead to encephali-tis, but I didn't find anything to suggest that encephalitis leads to mysti-cal experiences. In any case it seemed to me that no bio-chemical explana-tion gave me any real answer to the problem of meaning; it could only hope to describe the physiological basis. My conviction was, also, that my physiology, my biochemistry, at any one time, whether 'natural' or al-tered by illness and drugs, was necessarily part of me. Therefore I had to grapple with the meaning of it as part of my personal life, even if it had, apparently, no meaning for anyone else.

I had never received religious mythology in my home although I had a long-standing interest in mysticism and comparative religion. This ex-traordinary visit had come after a few weeks of being ill and suffering from insomnia and I had been using traditional spiritual practices, such as telling the rosary, rather intensely. So another part of me wanted a spir-itual 'explanation', especially as the aftermath of the visit was blissful and divine...so beatific, in fact, that I couldn't really deal with everyday life. I puzzled and debated with myself over the purpose of my encounter:

Gabriel

Why do you come in the dark night,
With a golden gown concealing the real light
Why cover your dangerous wings
With a feathered haze?
Now, tyrant, step from behind that Florentine countenance,
Remove that gentle, pallid mask,
And let me see your unrelenting face.

This poem expresses the frustration I felt. I was being haunted by re-calls of the visit and of the altered states of consciousness, the cosmic world that I had entered during the six weeks following it. In my medita-tions I would meet visual reminders, angels with iconographical faces, sometimes just shining mandalas in brilliant colours. In many ways I wanted to get on with an 'ordinary' life – I had married a few months after the experience, as the 'guidance' at the time had predicted. I wanted to be practical, get my house together, develop a lifestyle which fitted in with usual run of things – especially as the two children I had been bringing up alone had been unsettled by living with a mystical mother for a whole summer. So I organised my time around pragmatic tasks: I had been to art college and trained as a teacher, so I dabbled in dress design and part-time lecturing. When my intellect felt under-nourished I ran to the Open University for another course; this kept me away from the esoteric book-shop. And I had another baby. But the poems popped up here and there, provoking more thoughts, more questions.

I had been very lucky, during my weeks of inner voyaging, that my family had not turned me over to the medical profession, but had sup-ported me in my own home and helped with my children. I had two other things that supported me: firstly I knew more about mysticism than I did about madness and had an inner certainty that voices heard should be listened to but not, necessarily, discussed with non-believers. Secondly, I met a helper who was a Sufi and reinforced my own convictions; he also told me how to handle the demons who might raise their ugly heads in the wake of the angelic presence. Nonetheless I had been brought up in a rational household, without one iota of religious training, and when I came back to my everyday self the doubts crept in. Had it all been a product of temporary insanity, of an imagination overactivated by stress and loneliness?

To John Clare and all mad poets

Believe me, friend, you cannot understand
The mad worlds that entertain this mind,
Nor enter into the hurly-burly chaos
That spins in the gyroscopic brain.
Wild planets and myriads of startling stars
Explode and reappear within the cerebellum,
And only the first Creator has set
Constellations in higher orbs than mine.

I have clambered through celestial
Domes and crystal caverns, timeless in
Pale dominions, through uncharted seas and
Galaxies unbeknown to angel, man or god,
And stood untouched among the hurling
Golden hair of comets, and
Falling stars have brushed my eyelids

> *And crowned my hair with diadems of dew.*
> *And now that silence has descended,*
> *The voice of God no longer echoes in my ears,*
> *And the visions of His angels that entranced me*
> *Have faded in the cold blue light of day,*
> *Look upon me, that you might have called insane,*
> *As one who has danced unhindered through the heavens*
> *And now, regretfully, returns to earth,*
> *To feel once more the common touch of clay.*

One particular poem acted like the grit in the oyster. This one had been written eighteen months before the visitation. At that time I was not in the habit of writing poems at all. I had recently learned to meditate and it arrived, unbidden and whole in my head and I wrote it down, as though it had been dictated:

Dreamer

> *Am I a somnambulist*
> *In a world of waking dreams*
> *And patterns that we thrust*
> *Upon the universe?*
>
> *Shall I see beyond the shadows*
> *And the patterns on the screen,*
> *And find a brighter, clearer*
> *Vision to enhance them?*
>
> *Take my hand, mighty wizard,*
> *Holy priest, come with me,*
> *Through myself,*
> *That I may know and*
> *Be a part of Morning Glory.*

However often I tried to dismiss my experiences as temporary psychosis – and I am sure that this would have been the medical opinion if I had been subjected to too much scrutiny by that profession – there was an underlying nugget of certainty, one which I hardly dared to nurture, that I had indeed been given 'a brighter, clearer vision'. The continuing question was: how can this vision enhance the everyday world so that the world does not seem simply a shadowland by comparison? How can the presence of Morning Glory be brought into daily life so that it can be lived from moment to moment with a sense of joy and ecstasy? T.S. Eliot said that humankind cannot bear 'too much reality'. We close ourselves off from Eden in order to live the common-sense life and, when it becomes too common, too boring, we invent escapes into other worlds we create ourselves: television, novels, shopping malls. But we fear ecstasy – it is too demanding, it requires too much discipline and too much surrender. Occasionally we touch it, through meditation, dance, celebration, ritual and we are lit up, we become truly alive. Then we return to solid world and die again.

Another powerful issue was the question 'Why me?' My philosophy is that the universe is not chaotic but purposeful, that everything has meaning. In the beatific state that becomes a crystal clear certainty. In that state one becomes:

clothed with the heavens and crowned with stars: and perceive(s) (oneself) to be sole heir of the whole world Thomas Traherne, *Centuries of Meditation*, 1. 29

This experience is extremely dangerous for the wretched ego which is so susceptible to inflation. It was, no doubt, this experience that led poor James Naylor, one of the earliest Quakers, to ride into Bristol on a donkey while his friends waved palms. He was, needless to say, found guilty of heresy and cruelly tortured. But Traherne's meditation goes on:

...and more than so, because men are in it who are ev'ry one sole heirs, as well as you.

I knew that the famous mystics, such as Teresa of Avila, St. Paul, the prophet Mahomet, had described equally dramatic visitations. All of them have been put down by reductionists as abnormal in some way or another; Mahomet thought he was going mad himself and Islam may owe some gratitude to his wife who seems to have helped him stabilise the experiences. I had also known a man in Muswell Hill, the landlord of the house I lived in, go through a period of religious ecstasy which prompted him to stand on Muswell Hill at four in the morning, in his pyjamas, declaring that the Kingdom of Heaven was here and now. He was locked up, of course, and a few years later I saw him, deprived of all ecstasy, shuffling out from the gates of a mental hospital to collect cigarettes from a local shop. The twentieth century has no time or place for its mystics. On two counts I wanted to forget the experiences and be an everyday person: firstly I was determined to avoid the 'God has given me a message' syndrome (in any case, if It had, I didn't know what it was, so I would have been stuck there!), and secondly I wasn't going to let anyone give me electric shock treatment.

Nonetheless, I became aware that it was a rare experience: I had been taken to frontiers of consciousness which few people have the opportunity to explore unless they use drugs, in which case the experience is briefer (unless they ingest daily). I felt I had been privileged, but I found it impossible to share the experience and therefore felt that somehow I was alienated from other people. It is rather like being a woman who has birthed a child: if you talk to women who haven't yet had the experience there is a gap which can't be closed. The problem with trying to ignore such an experience is quite simply that you can't: for the astronauts who visit the moon that experience becomes central to their whole being. So it is with an experience of mystical intensity. It is certainly like a galactic journey: 'picking flowers from the galaxy' was Coleridge's phrase for his own travels.

Conqueror

I took the earth's ball in my hand
And climbed the pillars of the universe to stand
Crowned with drifting clouds.
And with my feet the oceans spanned.
Majestic...Still...Still.
Then, suddenly, and with triumphant roar,
Soared through the sunlight,
Through the star-bespattered night,
To stand amazed upon the earth once more.

The astronauts, of course, get fêted for their outer journeys, just as mystics of the past have been canonized for their inner travels. I had the distinct impression that few modern people are interested in tales of inner voyaging. But I also felt strongly that every human experience has significance and voyages to the moon or inner kingdoms need to be shared; they enrich the human consciousness at a deep level. I had no idea how I could share the experiences; I wrote poems which would seem too personal and subjective for publication and, apart from my husband, I never met anyone to whom I could even begin to describe my travels.

In 1981, after having my fourth daughter, we went to live near Glastonbury and I gave myself space to explore the inner world which had been sending the unwelcome messages for so long. The interior visions became stronger and clearer, some so detailed that I wanted to attempt paintings. The first of these was of an extraordinarily tall angel with a fiery headdress. Its gown was white but with an edging of green. It was walking in a country landscape and held in one hand an olive branch, in the other a blue crystal. The angel wore brown sandals, like a monk, and a lamb bounced at its heels. I felt that it was a guardian of the earth; the sandals showed that it had the possibility of actual involvement with the earth, and that, despite its power and sublimity, it was not out of our reach. The olive branch and the lamb indicated growth, new life, harmony. The crystal I was unsure about. I was not involved with crystals and never felt drawn to them. My feeling was that it acted in this picture as a symbol of basic structure; later I discovered it was also a visual pun from the collective unconscious.

This picture became the first clue to the adventures which have brought me to the writing of this book. My researches led me to discover that there was an Archangel called Sandalphon whose role was that of Guardian Spirit, who was associated with the earth and who stood at the foot of the Tree of Life. Sandalphon is one of the tallest creatures in the celestial realms. Moses called it 'the tall angel' and one of the Talmudic Haggia confirms that its head touches heaven. Sandalphon is said to be taller than any other angel by a journey of five hundred years.

I was now in a position where I felt certain that my inner world was offering me images which had some reference to the symbolic world provided by ancient Western traditions. My university studies had included the works of two remarkable visionaries who acted as mentors for me. The first was William Blake, whose certainty of the power, necessity and truth of the Divine Imagination inspired me on all those occasions when I doubted the validity of my own interior visions.

Blake realized that the rising empiricism of the natural sciences would relegate the imagination to the vagaries of a 'personalistic' inner world, without proper structure, foundation or reality. For him the imagination was neither vague, unreal nor 'merely subjective': on the contrary, it described a precise order of reality, pertaining to a definite mode of being with a coherent structure of its own...(he) affirmed the structural coherence of imagination, and rebelled against the tyranny of technical and mechanical reason which threatened the imaginative basis of all human experience.

Roger Cook, *The Tree of Life*, Thames and Hudson

I felt I had at least a scrap of evidence that the inner world has a proper structure and a foundation in reality, and that I could follow Blake's example and accept the visionary world as one worth exploring, and not dismiss it as 'merely subjective'.

My other mentor was that extraordinary personality Teresa of Avila, who understood the importance of standing by the truth of the intimate revelations available to the mystic, and that no church, or outside influence, should be allowed to undermine the certainty that accompanies the true vision. With these two giants and a couple of layman's books on the Kabbala, I set off on my travels through the interior. This book, therefore, is presented as a travelogue. It is not presented, however, simply as a descriptive journal of my own inner journey but as a traveller's guide and my intention is to provoke others to follow in my footsteps and those of mystics before me. In the past the mystical journey was undertaken by the recluse, by men and women who had detached themselves from the day to day world in order to explore the inner world. But now we are stand at the dawning of a Golden Age in which all God's people can be prophets; the great archetypal energies, known to the ancients as gods, devas or Archangels, are constantly present in creation throughout history, and are now urging us to make their acquaintance.

THE TREE OF LIFE

At the origin of things we are faced with an infinite containing a mass of unexplained finites; an indivisible full of endless divisions, an immutable teeming with mutations and differentiations, a cosmic paradox is at the beginning of all things. This paradox can only be explained as One, but this is an infinite Oneness which can contain the hundred and the thousand and the million and the billion and the trillion... This does not mean that the One is plural, or can be limited or described as the sum of the many. On the contrary, it can contain the infinite many because it exceeds all limitation or description by multiplicity, and exceeds at the same time all limitation by finite, conceptual oneness.

Sri Aurobindo, *The Life Divine*

If my inner adventures became curious when I moved to Glastonbury, they became curiouser and curiouser when I discovered that one particular inner vision had distinct characteristics linking it to the Archangel Sandalphon, who stands at the foot of the Kabbalistic Tree of Life, an iconographical scheme which claims to describe the metaphysics of the manifest universe. The book I was reading mentioned several other Archangels, including Gabriel, but some whose names were quite new to me. I wanted to learn more, but I felt that I should rely on my intuition rather than on the public library. It was certainly useful to look at a couple of basic books about the Tree of Life and the Kabbala, but I was anxious not to make an academic enquiry; I felt this might hinder the unfolding of the inner pictures which had initiated my curiosity in the first place.

The Tree of Life gave me a map and several 'place-names' and I thought I would explore further, using the map as my starting point. So at this stage in my account I shall pass on to you a minimum account of the Kabbalistic Tree of Life scheme. It is not intended to be a definitive treatise, just a basic grounding so that I can recount my encounters knowing that you share the same map.*

And so, Best Beloved, as the story goes, let us begin at the Beginning:

---

* If you want to read more see Bibliography, books 1 and 2. I should say here that my own explorations led me to some conclusions which do not fit the Kabbalist tradition - especially concerning the designation of various planets to the the Sefiroth. As I am not bound to the tradition I feel I can work with my own intuitive responses, rather than be bound to interpretations of the past. More on this in Appendix 2.

And out of the ground made the LORD God to grow every tree that is pleasant to sight, and good for food; the tree of life also in the midst of the garden, and the tree of the knowledge of good and evil.

Genesis 2:9.

While Adam and Eve lived in the Garden of Eden they were immortal; the Lord God filled the Garden with fruit which they could freely eat, including the fruit of the tree of life. The only forbidden fruit was that of the tree of knowledge of good and evil. Once they had disobeyed this prohibition God said:

'Behold, the man is become as one of us, to know good and evil: and now, lest he also put forth his hand, and take also of the tree of life, and eat, and live forever:'

Therefore the LORD God sent him forth from the garden of Eden, to till the ground from whence he was taken.

So he drove out the man; and he placed at the east of the gardens of Eden Cherubims, and a flaming sword which turned every way, to keep the way of the tree of life.

Genesis 3:22-24

It is important to note the content of this passage carefully: it clearly states that there are two trees in the Garden, one of Good and Evil and one of Life. The only limitation on Adam and Eve in the Garden was that they should not eat the fruit of the first tree, that of Good and Evil. So, we can assume, the fruit of the Tree of Life was freely available to them until they were banished and the flaming sword arrived for duty. This punishment is a symbol of the human condition: its consciousness condemned to duality and a thirst for the divine source of life, the memory of which provokes the imagination to create myths and symbols which perpetually harken back to the original state of innocence in the garden. The image of the tree as a model of divine order, fed from the deep source of cosmic creativity and manifesting in a coherent structure through root, bark, branch and leaf, subject to cycles of growth, fruition and decay, penetrating heaven, earth and underworld, is common to all the great creation myths. It is found in Genesis and in other ancient middle-Eastern imagery; it is found in Norse myths in which it is called Yggdrasil, on which Odin makes his sacrifice in order to be initiated into the cosmic mystery. The tree is a model of the sacred in Buddhism and in Hinduism, and in Islam, where imagery was discouraged, carpets are patterned, explicitly and implicitly, with the form and layout of the gardens of Paradise. The tree is found in the symbolic art of Java, Tibet, Thebes, Egypt, Assyria, Mexico, China, Japan; the Navaho Indians draw trees in the sand (with masculine zig-zags and feminine curves) and the great Sioux visionary Black Elk saw

a flowering stick... that was alive... and sprouted from the top and sent forth branches, and on the branches many leaves came out and murmured, and in the leaves the birds began to sing.

The Kabbalist's Tree of Life is not simply a metaphor or a symbol for the cycles of birth, growth and death, for which the tree is so obviously suited; it is a model which describes the underlying metaphysics of the created world. This description (which has a history that may date back to Abraham and is certainly evident in the construction of the Temple at the time of Solomon) seems to be remarkably accurate when held up for comparison with the discoveries of quantum physics.

One of the earliest works in the Kabbalist's library is the *Sepher Yitzerah* which reveals the philosophical construction of the Hebrew alphabet, ascribing to each letter a planet and a sign of the Zodiac. It also uses Pythagorean concepts of a triangle or trinity containing the ten letters relating to the name of God.

For if all things exist by [God's] eternal decrees, it is evident that in each species of things the number depends on the cause that produced it. There we find the first number, and thence it is come to us.

Now the finite interval of number is ten, for he who would reckon more than ten comes back to one, two, three, until, by adding the second decade, he makes twenty, by making the third decade in like manner he makes thirty, and so goes on by tens until he comes to an hundred. After a hundred he comes back again to one, two, three, and thus the interval of ten always repeated will amount to an infinity.

Hierocles commentary on the Golden Verses of Pythagoras

The process of movement from one, through eight stages to resolution in a tenth point from which the new movement begins is also echoed in an ancient Egyptian description in which Thoth says:

I am One which transforms into Two
I am Two which transforms into Four
I am Four which transforms into Eight
After all of this, I am One.

The Kabbalist's Tree describes this transformation from the initial impetus of creation, seen as a Crown at the top of the tree, unfolding through eight stages to resolve at the tenth stage, the Kingdom, at the base. Each stage is marked by a Sephira (a container is one possible translation for

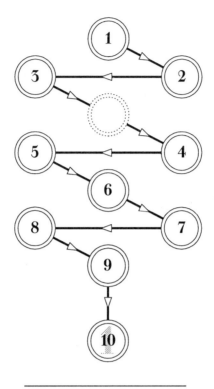

Figure 1 The lightning flash

this word); there are ten Sephiroth plus one 'non-Sephiroth' which is unseen or empty.

The Sephiroth, or Attributes of God, are organized into a specific archetypal pattern which provides a model on which everything that is to come into existence is based. Each Sephira in turn manifests under the influence of the divine energy which flows from a central point at the top, then left and right in a zig-zag to the foot of the tree. This movement is known as the lightning flash (see fig. 1).

For the Kabbalist God is beyond existence, transcendent: AYIN, meaning in Hebrew 'No Thing'. AYIN is Void, has no movement, no stillness, is neither above nor below, is nowhere; God is Absolute Nothing. Then God becomes Immanent, AYIN SOF, Absolute All. This is God everywhere, Alpha and Omega, infinite but having no Attributes because they can only manifest within existence, which is finite.

The oral tradition of the Kabbala tells us that 'God wished to behold God' and allowed the mirror of existence to appear in the void. In order to do this God withdrew the AYIN SOF, Absolute All, from one place in order to give space for manifestation. In other words there is an act of contraction — 'Zim-zum' — which permits duality and a dynamic creativity to take place, through which all that we experience can be manifested. The divine act of manifestation emanates from the AYIN SOF OR, the Endless Light which surrounds the void as a beam of light, the 'Kav' or beam of Divine Will, and manifests in ten distinct stages, the Sephiroth. This word has no equivalent in any other language but derives from the same root as the word 'cipher', i.e. a symbol or number. It is also the root of the word 'sapphire' — a brilliant blue stone.

The Sephiroth are sometimes described as the Divine Powers or Vessels, or as tools of Divine Governance. Some mystics visualise them as ten Hands or Faces, or Garments, of God. They express Divine Attributes, held eternally in a set of relationships until the Divine Will releases its own Act of Contraction and they vanish back into the Void.

The relationships between the Sephiroth are dictated by the 'Zahzahot', or Hidden Splendours. These are three Divine Principles —Will, Mercy and Justice. Will is the balancing principle, Mercy the principle of Expansion and Justice the principle of Constraint. The flow of Emanation begins its descent from a central point and then moves towards the right, touches the next Sephira, then back to the left, then back to the right, and so on. Thus the ten Divine Attributes are organized into a particular archetypal pattern.

The Tree is visualized as having three pillars – the central pillar of balance, or Equilibrium; an active, or masculine force on the right, the pillar of Mercy; and a passive, or feminine force, the pillar of Justice, on the left. The Zahzahot starts at the top, on the central pillar, at a point called 'Keter', Crown; to the right it touches the top of the pillar of Mercy at 'Hokhmah', Wisdom; moving back to the left it touches the top of the pillar of Justice at 'Binah', Understanding. As it moves back towards the right pillar it touches the central pillar at a point of balance called 'Daat', Knowledge. This is the place of the Holy Spirit, Ruah ha Kodesh, which has a place within manifestation although it remains unmanifest: 'the empty room'. Daat hovers as a veil below the three 'supernal' Sefiroth and is considered to be a place where the Absolute may enter and intervene directly with existence. The next point it touches is 'Hesed', Mercy, on the right pillar, then back to the left pillar for 'Gevurah', Judgement. Then it crosses the central pillar again at 'Tiferet', Beauty, as it moves down to the last point on the right pillar, 'Nezah', Eternity or Victory. The return to the left pillar meets 'Hod', Reverberation or Glory, then the lightning flash makes two final moves down the central pillar to 'Yesod', Foundation, and 'Malkhut', Kingdom (see fig. 2, overleaf).

We can see that the act of creation involves a structure, an archetypal

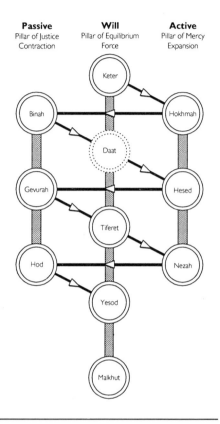

Passive
Pillar of Justice
Contraction

Will
Pillar of Equilibrium
Force

Active
Pillar of Mercy
Expansion

Figure 2   The pillars of the Tree of Life

process which is fired by an initial dynamic and proceeds through eight stages until it is complete.

The metaphor of the lightning flash indicates that we can regard the Tree of Life as a system of functioning rather like an electrical circuit, through which flows a divine current. Any one Sefirah can change the direction of flow, creating a variety of fields and actions. The power available to all of them can be increased or decreased, thus modifying results, events or manifested output, but the current always is earthed at Malkhut. Thus the Kabbalist creates a model which demonstrates the metaphysical structure of all existence; the Sefiroth are the basic components, three are aligned on the right-hand pillar of Mercy; three on the passive left-hand Pillar of Severity and four (plus the non-Sefirah Daat) on the central pillar of Equilibrium or Grace. Their relationships, initiated by the path of the lightning flash, are further developed by a total of twenty two paths which correspond to each of the letters of the Hebrew alphabet* (see fig. 3).

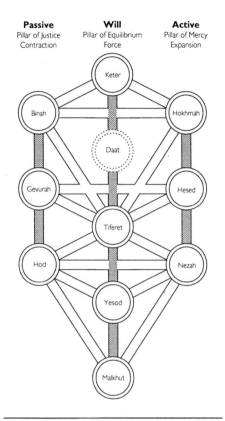

Passive	Will	Active
Pillar of Justice	Pillar of Equilibrium	Pillar of Mercy
Contraction	Force	Expansion

Figure 3   The pillars of the Tree of Life

The Tree of Life model can be seen as a divine building block, God's Lego, which interlocks over and over again at different levels of energy, from the most subtle to the most material (see fig. 4, overleaf). This structure underlies any complete being, organization or creative process, yet it never stands alone; it is never sufficient to itself because one creation always leads to another; the roots of one tree become the crown of the next just as the Doh at the bottom of a musical octave becomes top Doh for the next octave; alpha and omega are one and

In my end is my beginning. T. S. Eliot, *East Coker*

We can thus look at each point on the Tree of Life as an archetype, a

---

*   I have not marked the letters on the figure shown here, since they are not important for our use. The Kabbalistic system is quite complex and I have used the bare bones for my purpose.

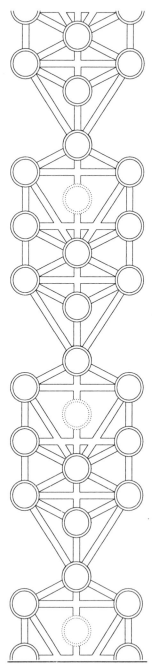

Figure 4 God's Lego set

function in creation, taking equal and necessary part in a Divine Process. These functions govern and shape creation, both seen and unseen. The names for the Sephiroth indicate their function in the process, but these functions are at a purely abstract level and we need a bridge of communication in order to receive any understanding of them. This is the task of the Archangel, to be a cognitive link between the pure, unknowable energy of the Sefiroth and the human mind. We can imagine the Tree as having ten roses of immeasurable light on it and as the petals of these flowers open each reveals a winged figure, an intelligence on a subtle level; it has no physical form, but its wings symbolize its ability to communicate with our own intelligence which is indeed governed by the same underlying process (see fig. 5).

Some of the angelic names are familiar to us, particularly those who occupy some of the lower branches, and the tradition of Western religious art has equipped us to summon up visualizations — especially of Gabriel, Michael and Raphael. I was always vaguely aware that there were seven Archangels and that they probably corresponded in some way to the seven planets. I was surprised to discover ten and that a couple of the names were not of Hebrew origin but, apparently, Greek. I was delighted to find Sandalphon at the foot of the tree, because his name, and what little I could discover about him, indicated that my own vision linked with Western tradition of the Archangels. The blue crystal was the visual clue... sapphire has the same root as Sephira.

The Kabbalist sees the whole of the manifest Universe as one vast Tree of Life and that all the created things within the Universe are structured in the same way: a human body, or a cell from that body or the proverbial grain of sand. The microcosm is an identical reflec-

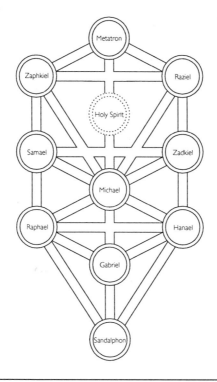

Figure 5 The Archangels on the Tree of Life

tion of the macrocosm; every atom of Creation is based on the same metaphysical model. The Tree is understood to function at four different levels called the four worlds, which correspond to the four symbolic states of matter, the elements of fire, air, water and earth. These levels descend from the top of the Tree:

the world of Emanations — Atziluth (Fire)

the world of Creations — Briah (Air)

the world of Formations — Yetzirah (Water)

the world of Action — Asiyyah (Earth)

However, the worlds penetrate each other as a natural part of the creative process, so that their Trees are seen to overlap. Each world has its own complete Tree within itself. Thus the Malkhut of the Atziluthic world is also the Tiferet of Briah world, layering down to the lowest Malkhut where the residue of all the worlds is concentrated. In human beings these worlds correspond to the Platonic bodies:

27

the spiritual or divine body
the rational body
the emotional or subtle body
the physical body

The world of Atziluth is the realm in which the Tree of Life is in its purest state, it is close to the Endless Light. Its three Sephiroth are those at the top of the tree and are directly in contact with the Divine. The three equivalent Archangels, Metatron, Zaphkiel and Raziel, are known as the 'Holy Spirits of the Face'. In the Book of Tobit the Archangel Raphael speaks of himself as 'one of the seven who stand before the throne', as though the three Archangels who sit here, beyond the veil of Daat, are separated from the seven on the lower branches, 'in light inaccessible, hid from our eyes'. But in the grand scheme of the Universe the Divine uses the point of Daat to intervene and then the next world, of Briah, is activated.

Briah is quintessentially the realm of the Archangels - they are creatures of air, communicators. They provide the bridge between the world of spirit and the worlds of form and substance. Their own world is also a tree structure, and our ability to receive communications from them tends to relate to the lower worlds of their tree, which is why we are more familiar with the names of Gabriel, Raphael and Mikael than those of the Archangels in the higher worlds. I came to understand that my extraordinary visitation had opened a gateway into the angelic realms and that I was now being invited through the gate by Sandalphon.

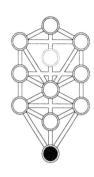
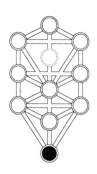

1

SANDALPHON

THE GUARDIAN

Not where the wheeling systems darken,
And our benumb'd conceiving soars! -
The drift of pinions, would we hearken,
Beats at our own clay-shutter'd doors.

The angels keep their ancient place;
Turn but a stone, and start a wing!
'tis ye, 'tis your estranged faces,
That miss the many-splendoured thing.

Frances Thomson, *In No Strange Land*

I was brought up in the Oxfordshire countryside at a time when rural roads were rarely invaded by motor cars. Our home was part of an isolated community a couple of miles from a very small village, ten miles from the nearest market town and twenty from the city. Buses were limited and we had no transport of our own. A van took me to school and back but otherwise I walked. I had little company and spent much time wandering 'lonely as a cloud' down narrow lanes and over hills. I was an imaginative child and I liked my own company. My relationship with nature was not at all scientific: I was not interested in collecting and identifying plants or hunting insects, I just took a delight in the presence and the beauty, and a sense of belonging to something magical. I knew there were fairies hiding everywhere but I never saw them except with the inner eye. Then, as now, such intuitive vision was dismissed as 'only your imagination'. 'Only!', I hear William Blake protest.

My imagination was a useful resource at times; I easily wrote stories and collected high marks and prizes for English. I applied it to writing a school play and making costumes; later I went to art college and afterwards worked as a dress designer. But I was always unsure of my relationship with my imagination; the message seemed to be that it can lead you into trouble and that day-dreaming is time-wasting and ineffectual. What practical use has it? The fairy-tale realm is for children only; they are expected to 'grow out' of it. For adults it is potentially dangerous; although great artists may enter it, they are rarely left unscathed. In any case, artists are generally reputed to be more than a little off their trolley. My own absent father was presented as an example to me of someone, highly intelligent but ungrounded, who had drifted into the smoke rings of Wonderland and had lost touch with what most people called reality. This was the great difficulty for me; the intense mystical experiences I had took me headlong into a separate reality and I knew it was impossible to live a balanced life if one stayed in it. But I was also certain that it contained wonders that needed to be explored; I wanted a foot in both realities. Was that possible? Where did I start?

I started, eventually, in the Somerset countryside, not far from Glastonbury. It certainly isn't necessary to live in the countryside in order to make inward journeys, but it does help. There are still quiet spaces and there can be solitude, if you give yourself the time. An unsuccessful business venture put me and my husband in the position to follow up a yearning to live near Glastonbury and we found a house to rent at the foot of the Polden Hills. We had a small baby who gave me the excuse I needed to go for walks down country lanes, just as I had when I was small.

One day I was returning to the house along the edge of the main road which carves through the landscape at the foot of Pedwell Hill. This road runs to Taunton and can be very busy at certain times of the day. But when there is no traffic the atmosphere is very quiet. The residents in the few houses of Pedwell are either at work, or hiding in their gardens and kitchens, and there is no shop to encourage idle gossipers. I trundled the pushchair along the tarmac, thinking mainly about a cup of tea, but also enjoying the peace. Quite suddenly the atmosphere seemed charged with some extraordinary power. My hands and feet began to tingle. I stopped. There was a sense that a vast presence was hanging in the air. I held my breath. It felt like an ancient power, a god of the hills rising from his green bed. What would I see if I turned? Someone... some thing... a colossus stretching itself up and up from the earth and reaching into the clouds. It seemed as though it was a guardian, a protector of the landscape, watching the mortal goings-on with a piercing eye. I felt very, very small. I decided not to turn around. I didn't feel threatened, just awe-inspired. Part of me welcomed the presence, the rest of me felt it was much too big for a mere mortal to deal with. So I gathered my senses together and began, very slowly indeed, to finish my journey to the house.

It was many months later that the inner vision of Sandalphon presented itself to me. I made a feeble attempt to paint the picture, and it was some time before I discovered that there was an Archangel who fitted my description. More time elapsed before I realized that the experience in Pedwell and the picture were connected. In traditional Kabbala each Sefiroth — and, therefore, each Archangel — is associated with one of the planets. Sandalphon is the Archangel of the Earth and this concept seemed to fit my experience.

The name Sandalphon is derived from the Greek. The first part means what it says, sandal. 'Phon', as in 'telephone', means voice. Perhaps: 'the sound of sandals'. I had thought the sandal bit of my vision quite incongruous; plain monkish brown leather straps over the feet seemed mundane when the angel had such glorious wings and a vast halo. But this character is grounded in the earth and participates in its cycles and evolution. On the Tree of Life it stands at the foot, on the Sephira Malkhut - the kingdom. It guards the natural world and facilitates the legions of angels and fairies which function within it. The physical body of Mother Earth and her spirit twin, the Moon,* are its domain and its responsibility. Its presence can be felt everywhere, even in cities where man's presence seems to be in command. When we left Somerset we moved to Plymouth where we lived in a long street of houses with no trees. We had no garden to speak of, but I could still find the Archangel:

Angel

If they ask me 'Where is this angel that you claim to see?'
I shall answer them with certainty.
I see it in the raindrops on my window pane,
I see it in the sky, even on this grey day.
And when the heavens are blue and my heart is lifted,
I hear its song the louder, I see its halo is sharper,
It will not be ignored.

I see it in the light that catches rooftops,
Glistening on the drab, grey battleships, the steel cranes,
The artefacts in the dockyard, the sprawling houses on the hill.
It washes over moorland, granite, peat,
And fills my little yard with newness and with hope.

Its power pervades the shameless weed
That penetrates the concrete paving stones,
And throws a lilac haze across the dwellings,
Burned and bombed, tenements once filled
With cries and now deserted.

---

* According to the Kabbala, Gabriel is the Archangel of the Moon, but my experiences led me to feel otherwise. I shall develop this theme later in the chapter on Gabriel.

Sandalphon: The Guardian

It flames the scarlet pyracantha,
It roars the yellow dandelion,
Swings the skirt of columbine,
Meditates the stiff lily,
Blushes in the eros of the rose.

In the velvet night I feel it.
The air is full, the owl knows it,
And the clawed mouse as he surrenders.
Quiet creatures of the damp earth,
Blind of eyes, sharp of smell,
Crawling things from the witches vat,
Earthworm, woodlouse, newt and toad —
Each one fulfils the angel's bidding
And dances to a song they fail to hear.

It fills the bed where lovers sleep,
Male and female, damp armpits, moist legs.
Stirs in the deep womb, fires the meeting cells,
Stretches the white belly, fills the breast,
Drives the infant in its journey to the air.

I am angry that they cannot see the angel.
I am angry that their eyes are shuttered
And their senses closed. This is why
Our mother, earth, is weeping,
Why forests fall and dolphins die.
Do they call the human 'homo sapiens'?
How can a man be wise who cannot see
That angels move among us every moment,
Bidding us to share eternity.

Sandalphon is the Archangel on whom we should call in matters that concern the future of our planet. Which brings me to the very important issue of the relationship between man and the Archangels. We tend to be in awe of the angelic tribes; they seem to be all fire and air and we are entrenched in baser elements. We see them as something to aspire to; the façade of Bath Abbey depicts a ladder of stone at the foot of which mere mortals begin their climb to heaven, growing wings as they near the top. This is a stereotypical image of the evolutionary process, the higher you get the less material you become, therefore the angels are superior to humankind, elevated beings on a spiritual plane and we should be jolly privileged to make contact with them. But if we return to the original story of the Creation, we find this little sub-plot: after man was created God tells all the angelic hosts, including the big chiefs, the Archangels, to submit to the service of mankind. This command was flouted by Satan who claimed that if it loved God it couldn't possibly demean itself to serve a mere mortal made in God's image. Satan was then given the boot by Michael, Commander in Chief of Archangels: *me thou hast created of smokeless fire, and shall I reverence a creature made of dust?**

It is commonly thought that Satan is the same character as Lucifer. This misconception is based on a quotation from Isaiah14:12: 'How art thou fallen from heaven, O Lucifer, son of the morning'. But Isaiah was using the epithet 'day-star' to describe the King of Babylon who proudly boasted that he would ascend to heaven and make himself equal with God, but who was fated to be cast down. This epithet was later translated as 'Lucifer' and St. Jerome and the Early Fathers applied the same name, by inference, to Satan. Poets, particularly Milton in 'Paradise Lost', have taken up this theme, leading to the incorrect assumption that Lucifer is an alternative name for Satan, whereas Lucifer means 'light-giver' and applies to the morning or evening star, Venus. Gustav Davidson, in his *Dictionary of Angels*, points out that the authors of the books of the Old Testament knew nothing of fallen or evil angels, and do not mention them, although in the Book of Job — 4.18 — the Lord 'put no trust' in his angels and 'charged them with folly'. Also in the Book of Job Satan appears before the Lord, alongside 'the sons of God' and the Lord does not rebuke him, but converses with him about the merits of the faithful servant, Job. God then permits Satan to take on the role of tester — the Hebrew word 'Satan' translates as adversary or enemy. In Numbers 22:22 the Lord stands against Balaam 'for an adversary' — 'satan'.

In Islamic tradition we find 'Shaitan', a fallen angel, also known as Iblis or Eblis, and we find the story of his disobedience in Surah 18 v 48: 'When We said to the angels "Prostrate yourselves before Adam," all prostrated themselves except Satan who was a jinnee disobedient to his Lord.'

Once humankind had also been given the boot, out of Eden, our capacity to make contact with the angels was reduced, we had shifted ourselves from a realm in which all was provided into one in which we had to fend for ourselves. Uncertain of our relationship with the natural world, whether it was kind and nurturing or uncertain and threatening, we armed ourselves with fear and grew to depend on our five senses. Always looking outward, concentrating on finding the next meal or dodging 'enemies'

---

*   This story is found in the Apocryphal book *Adam and Eve* and is quoted in *The Legends of the Jews* 1.63 by Louis Ginzberg (published 1954 by The Jewish Publication Society of America).

(other creatures or humans as frightened as ourselves), we grew into prag-matic, often aggressive beings with only vague recollections of a Garden in which everything had been lovely and angels served us in every corner. We can understand from this story that the creative intention was that the angels and Archangels are part of the support system. They belong to the world of Air, which emerged from the world of Fire, but they are a foun-dation for the worlds of Water and Earth. We are permitted to call on the angels; they were instructed to serve us. We therefore have the possibility of communicating with the invisible and being involved, at a metaphysi-cal level, with the unfolding of the material world.

This is the process which the founders of Findhorn entered into: a crea-tive dialogue with the underlying intelligence in the natural world. This is what happens when we talk to plants and do spiritual healing. It is essen-tial that we continue to explore the angelic world so that we can be in-volved in what the Kabbalist calls the work of unification. When we enter into this relationship with the invisible we are acknowledging our place within the scheme of things: the human being is an essential part of the plot but it is human vanity to assume that we have the exclusive use of 'intelligence', or that we can manipulate the natural world without due consideration of Divine Intention. Talking with angels will not give more manipulative power; it will give us a chance to participate in the real dy-namics of creation. Our participation will lead to a smoother transition in our own evolution and we will, once again, be able to live in Eden — as fully-fledged, wise humans and not as the infants we once were, who could not understand that the rules that are made are necessary for har-mony and balance. Sandalphon has guardianship for the earth and we need to co-operate with it in order to heal our planet as well as our own, self-inflicted, wounds. This is a simultaneous task to be undertaken on the inner and outer levels; every small step we take in the right direction will be rewarded by an increase in our sense of joy and harmony at being involved in creation.

My vision of Sandalphon was set in an English pastoral scene but it can be envisioned in every possible place: I can see it in snow-peaked moun-tains and in Equatorial jungles, on bleak moorland and in the desert. When the Soil Association saw the success of the Findhorn garden they were amazed at such growth from such poor soil, like sand... but if we tune into the metaphysical we can align ourselves with an infrastructure of energies which are potent and transformative, and then a little matter of the quality of the soil is no limitation to the creation of a wonderful garden.

We need to remember that while Sandalphon is the Archangel for our world it is only one Archangel, at the foot of a whole tree. Its energy is dependent on the flow emanating from the top, moving from point to point, carrying the divine energy downwards. Every atom of our planet contains such a pattern. Sandalphon is the first point of communication, but we shall have more encounters before we can achieve any real sense of integration with ourselves and with our environment.

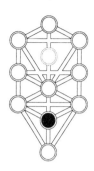

2

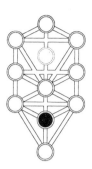

GABRIEL

THE MESSENGER

And it came to pass, when I, even I Daniel, had seen the vision, and sought for the meaning, then, behold, there stood before me as the appearance of a man.

And I heard a man's voice between the banks of Ulai, which called, and said, 'Gabriel, make this man to understand the vision.'

Daniel 8:15–16

I stand at the foot of the tree, in the kingdom: the presence and vision of Sandalphon have presented themselves with no request on my part but now, I feel, I have to venture onward of my own volition. It is as though someone has given me the first piece of paper in a treasure trail: the clue maker has offered me a possibility but no further clues will come my way without some request from me.

The traditional diagram of the Tree of Life informs me that the next Sephira is Yesod, Foundation, and that the Archangel for this vessel is Gabriel. The name 'Gabriel' means 'man-god'*. However, the Bible uses the word 'man' generically, to mean human rather than particularly male. Angels have no bodies and therefore no sexuality. The Archangels present themselves in a variety of vibrations, some of which may seem to us to be masculine, some feminine — for example, the healing vibration of Raphael may feel feminine while the constant creative drive of Hanael may seem masculine; but this is our interpretation based on social, historical and cultural conditioning.

Gabriel is well known to all of us because of its appearance at the Annunciation of the Virgin Mary. Less well known to Christians is the fact

---

* The suffix 'el' as in 'Elohim' — an alternative Hebrew name for Yahweh. We should note though that in Hebrew, 'Elohim' can be singular or plural, masculine or feminine, thus indicating the oneness and the multiplicity of the Divine and its inclusiveness of gender.

that Gabriel initiated the writing of the Koran by visiting the Prophet Mahomet (on whom be peace). Mahomet also makes a spiritual journey under Gabriel's guidance: he was taken to seventh heaven on an animal with the face of a man, the cheeks of a horse which had the wings of an eagle, its eyes were as brilliant as stars and it glittered all over with radiant light. The Arabic name for this creature is Al Borak, which means 'lightening': this seems to be a strong connection with the Kabbalist's lightning flash. Gabriel takes Mahomet up the same path into the higher realms of the tree.

Islamic tradition tells us that Mahomet was unlettered and he may have been actually illiterate, but more likely this means he was not already a scholar or a writer. We can see that in both cases Gabriel intervenes with a state of purity and simplicity and provokes the creation of something new, divinely inspired. Jesus is regarded as the Divine Word incarnate and the Koran as the Word of God. Man and book are both messages, in one way or an other, brought from the invisible world into human consciousness in order to transform human life.

In the Book of Daniel the prophetic vision is explained by Gabriel: here the angel has an intellectual function, interpreting raw data. Daniel describes himself as being 'in a deep sleep' and says that Gabriel set him upright — as though the vision is received in a trance state and the mental activity has to be re-instated in order for him to process it. Gabriel is the messenger *par excellence*. He may also be the same character as the ubiquitous 'Angel of the Lord' who is constantly delivering messages in the Old and New Testaments. Although I suspect that Gabriel employs a junior for some of the minor messages and is mainly present for major, history altering events. At this point of 'Foundation' Gabriel provides a pivot in the material world and is able to trigger action at a deep level: this action will be conception of one kind or another: a child, a painting or a book will emerge. Only the Archangels on the central pillar can take on a role in transforming the material world and the humans in it — perhaps this is why we are so much more aware of the activities of Gabriel and Michael, both of whom participate in our most famous angel stories. At this point on the tree the emanations are directly channelled into a single strand, reaching downwards to the kingdom, so at this stage the energy is gathered together for its final rush of creativity. If you are setting out to write, or to conceive, you need to make contact with Gabriel.

My vision of Sandalphon had arrived spontaneously and I was nervous about calling up a vision of Gabriel self-consciously. I felt that my knowledge of art history and the cultural impressions that I had inherited would get in the way of a genuine insight. I also had it in my mind that my 1974 visitation was connected with Gabriel and that I might get psychically flattened once more! I need not have worried on the latter score — I was wrong about that particular visitor. But Christmas card tableaux and Italian frescoes did interfere, initially, with me reaching a dynamic impression of Gabriel. At first I saw him in Renaissance cloisters, sitting at a desk with a quill pen in a scholastic hand, scratching away at an illuminated book. His garments were elaborately trimmed and the wings were very swanlike. My approach to the vision was to say to myself... 'Well, maybe... but we're not there yet.' Gradually, over a period of several weeks, during which I occasionally checked out the picture during my meditations, I came closer to what I felt was a truly living, vibrating impression of the Archangel Gabriel.

The 'face' of an Archangel is pure light; the impression of form which we receive says more about us, the receivers, than of the angel itself, although there are different vibrations which create certain kinds of responses in our senses. We react to them by 'seeing' different colours and patterns. Since the angelic world has no extension there is no actual, measurable form — what we see are patterns of dynamic energies collected into different harmonics, vibrating at different speeds. The images of the Archangels as beings are denser towards the foot of the tree because we are able to relate to these particular vibrations more easily; we are more aware of the way they manifest in our lives. As we ascend there seems to be less and less 'form' and what we 'see' becomes closer to pure light.

The Gabriel I saw was less human in appearance than Sandalphon. That is to say it seemed to be rather bodiless and had no feet. It hovered in a brilliant blue sky and its gown was a breathtaking white which sparkled, as though it was made of some kind of crystal. The 'feathers' on the 'wings' vibrated in an even rhythm, occasionally flashing in different colours, as though some kind of turning prism was shining on them. There seemed to be an emphasis on cool colours, blues, greens, turquoise. The halo of light radiated in golden shining lines from the head shape and from the area of the face where a mouth might be poured a stream of golden shapes, which seemed to be words and letters, written in languages I did not recognize. There was music, the nearest equivalent in human sounds that I know is a flute. It held a vast shining globe and when I came close I could see my own face reflected back to me.

I was fascinated by the constantly flowing stream of words and letters which poured from this being. The visual impression of jumbled shapes seemed to harmonise with the flute-like sound and I began to think that one could easily move into the flow and participate in it. Then one might write poetry in the way Shakespeare wrote, or music like Mozart. A number of pieces of poetry I have written myself seem to have arrived complete in my head, as though they had already been written before I noticed them and put pen to paper. Mozart is reputed to have said that he wrote down what he heard, and most of his manuscripts are uncorrected. Perhaps the creative genius, by setting aside his own, everyday 'persona', is able to surrender to the fluid imagination of Gabriel and open to the sounds of the cosmos. Nonetheless there is bound to be some input from the artist: the light pours into a vessel which is historically and culturally situated and these factors will colour the result. The Gabriel in each of us will recognize this divine music or poetry as archetypal and this is why such great artists become immortal.

For the Kabbalist, Gabriel is the Archangel of the Moon and we can see why that association has come about: the Annunciation is a very lunar occasion and distinctly feminine. But Gabriel could also be associated with Mercury, since he acts as a messenger for the Divine and I felt this to be a more comfortable association. I could see why the Moon would be the most obvious contender — for earlier visionaries the Moon was physically the first visible luminary to be viewed from Earth and the most obvious. But we know that the Moon is harnessed within the Earth's circuit and is intrinsically engaged with the rhythms of our own planet and I gradually began to feel a very powerful intuition that we should regard her as the Earth's Bride, or mystic sister, rather than as a completely separate archetype (see Appendix One on Auriel).

I think it is worth looking at a couple of other mythological messagebearing characters to expand our understanding of Gabriel, to see whether there is any other archetypal information that will throw light on its role on the tree.

Mercury is the Roman version of the Greek god Hermes, messenger of the gods. One of the roles he played was that of 'psychopompos', leader of souls, escorting the dead to the otherworld. Gabriel has also been referred to as the angel of death — in the Talmud he appears as the destroyer of hosts at Sennacharib:

For the Angel of Death spread his wings on the blast,
And breathed in the face of the foe as he pass'd;
And the eyes of the sleepers wax'd deadly and chill,
And their hearts but once heaved, and for ever grew still!

Byron, *The Destruction of Sennacharib*

Talmudic tradition also says that Gabriel is one of the angels who buries Moses. In Norse mythology the Germanic god Odin, whose day is Wednesday — Mercredi — is known as 'father of the slain'. It seems as though several mythologies recognize that the messenger of the gods plays a transformative role, taking as well as giving, and acting as guide for the human soul. This would seem an appropriate role at this point on the tree: the soul is leaving Malkhut, the earthly kingdom, and being drawn back into the upper vibrations of the tree. The next Sephira contacted will be at Yesod, where Gabriel can be found. People who have near death experiences inform us that they arrive at a point where a choice can be made whether to return to the body or not. This element of choice would be in keeping with the themes which astrologers associate with Mercury.

Communication and language are also Mercurial functions and Gabriel seems to appear in connection with writing (the Koran), interpreting visions (Daniel) and delivering messages (the Annunciation). One reference I found said that it is traditionally the only Archangel who can speak Syriac and Chaldee!

Western mythology offers us another winged visitor: the Greek Eros, a beautiful but wanton boy armed with arrows of desire. We find him, in a debased form, as the chubby cherub on the Valentine card. He was the son of Aphrodite, or Venus, the goddess of Love and his role is to inspire others with desire. Popularly 'desire' is thought of as meaning sexual desire but all creativity is initiated by desire, not all of which is carnal. Love is an essential ingredient in creation; the initiator must, in the best sense, be enamoured, otherwise his product will be less than perfect and his interest in completing the task will fall away. Thus we have the image of the arrows which 'fire' the artist or the lover with enthusiasm. In Hindu literature we find Kama, a brilliantly adroit youth, who arose at the creation of the universe and was first-born of the gods. He is described as 'ananga', bodiless, which fits my perception of Gabriel; he also represents desire, which is understood as the primal germ of the universal mind; without desire nothing is manifested. All these variations seem to have a common theme: there is desire, which is not simply sensual or human desire but a drive towards new goal. There is a message, a catalyst — a surprise turning around of an existing situation, this may mean falling in love or creating something unexpected; there is a dramatic change in one's relationship with the world. In this process Gabriel acts as the pivot; his presence allows the human mind to receive the information — though the original impetus has come from further up the line, so to speak. This dynamic fires the germ of the imagination and creativity begins.

According to the Sufi Jili, humanity is more central on the cosmic tree than the angels because we occupy the Kingdom, at the bottom of the tree, which is its axis. We are at the foot of a great trunk which rises straight upwards to the Crown of the Tree. The Angels are fixed at the points established by the various Sephiroth, according to the Divine plan of the creation, but humanity, created in the Divine 'image', has been given intuitive and imaginative knowledge of all the names of the Angels and is capable of climbing the Tree.

A key image in literature concerning the mystical progress of the soul is the ladder: the link with the tree is obvious and the concept of climbing towards a higher goal is contained in both images. In the famous dream of Jacob (Genesis 28:12) the patriarch sees a ladder stretching between earth and heaven, with angels ascending and descending on it. In the *Symposium*, Plato speaks of using examples of beauty in this world 'as steps to ascend continually with that absolute beauty as one's aim'. In the poems of the Sufi mystic Ibn' Arabi, a pulpit is used as a symbol of 'the ladder of the Most Divine Names'. To climb this ladder is to be invested with the qualities of these Names. In the same way we can climb the Tree of Life, both inwardly and outwardly. As we climb we meet the Archangels and each one opens a mysterious door in our own psyche, through which we can both see and receive. What can we see when we meet Gabriel? And what can we receive? We are in contact with a potent creative force, what writers call a muse or a daemon... I used the word 'unrelenting' in my own poem and when this energy enters your life it will not be gainsaid. It is not in the communication mechanism that Gabriel is to be found, but in the inspiration. You are more likely to find him in a jamming session where musicians improvise than in a concert hall where composed music is played. You will not find him in an art gallery where people simply admire that which has already been created, but in the studio where the painter is still grappling with his vision. You will not find him in the library where the words are now so much black ink on the paper, but in the writer's den, probably at four of the morning — and it never sleeps, despite what the author with writer's block may think. The music score, the painting and the books are all part of the Kingdom, they belong to the realm of Sandalphon; the realm of Gabriel precedes this, impregnating the human mind with the desire to create.

Gabriel's station, like those of the other Archangels, is fixed; its task is initiated at the top and has descended from the Crown by stages on the three pillars. This Archangel may have instructions to arouse desire in us but it contains no desire of its own: the lightning flash of energy from the Divine has already travelled through seven processes before it has arrived at Gabriel and each of those stages has contributed to the message which it delivers. If you intend to open yourself to creative possibilities, bear this in mind: unless you have some understanding of the whole process and have your feet well anchored in the Kingdom you may find yourself with a Pandora's box, brimming with images from the hidden world which you cannot handle. You must be prepared to be self-disciplined at the ground level if you wish to handle the treasures from heaven.

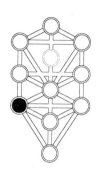

3

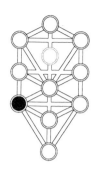

RAPHAEL

THE HEALER

Raphael, the sociable spirit that deigned
To travel with Tobias, and secured
His marriage with the seven-times-wedded maid.

Milton, *Paradise Lost*, V, 221

At this point on my tree map it seemed as though I had a choice: I could move to the right and visit Hanael, or to the left and visit Raphael. I felt a little like Alice when she stood at the cross-roads wondering whether to visit the Mad Hatter or the March Hare!

Raphael's name is not as well known as that of Gabriel's but there are some stories to glean from, so left seemed like the best option. I then realized that one doesn't really have a choice: taking a right turn would mean travelling up the tree in the opposite direction from the original, descending, path. This seemed appealing at first, since one would then create a double helix pattern around the central pillar. I came to the conclusion, however, that this was simply contrary and that the best route for the tourist in heaven was to follow the route that had already been carved out. (There are of course many small paths by which the energies within the Tree can interact, but I am speaking here of the path which has been established by the lightning flash, the 'hot-line', so to speak, the inter-city direct route between heaven and earth.) It also registered that this might well be the reason that Raphael was more accessible, because the Sephira Hod is the next obvious station stop for the traveller and this may be why Raphael has had more opportunities for contacting humanity.

In the Apocryphal Book of Tobit the archangel Raphael travels, disguised as a pilgrim, with Tobias into Media and back again, instructing him on the way to marry Sara and driving away the wicked spirit which has ruined seven marriages for her. Raphael also guides Tobias in healing his father's eyesight by showing him how to catch a miraculous fish and use part of its gut as a healing unction. When Tobias turns to thank his travelling companion the angel reveals himself as 'Raphael, one of the seven spirits before the throne'. It is this story which inspires Milton to call Raphael 'sociable' and 'affable'. This archangel is engaged in human activity and may be in disguise -unlike Gabriel whose visitations cannot possibly go un-remarked!

Raphael's name is translated as Divine Physician. The healing role, together with the companionship, seem to indicate a feminine vibration — which is appropriate for this point on the tree, the first that I had visited on the left, passive, pillar.

The only image of Raphael I had collected from art history was one of the angel in pilgrim's garb, quite wingless and not at all ethereal. So I had no preconception as to what I might meet when I found this character. I had developed a technique for making contact with the Archangels: I would visualize the tree as a block of flats with a series of stairways and corridors. Then I could find a front door for each Archangel. When I started I would ask, either can I come in, or will the inhabitant kindly step outside? I soon learned that I could not expect an Archangel to step outside its station, rather like the guards at Buckingham Palace they are obliged to stay in their allotted positions.

My first impression of Raphael was of delicate colours: lilac and lavender, soft pinks and grey; pale sunset wash colours, very fluid with a whispy, misty, texture. There was a sensation of being gently wrapped in a light-as-thistledown garment, by something that was caring and compassionate. The sounds were of light strings, hardly touched, like an Aeolian harp in the gentlest of breezes. When I looked for a face I found a shining head crowned with pink roses; the eyes seemed to be closed and the 'lashes' were golden rays streaming downwards. The lilac colours merged into a haze of wings and feathers, and the pink became a shining ribbon on which floated the words: 'I am the river of Divine Healing, flowing over the earth.'

This encounter was extraordinarily soothing. I felt as though I was in contact with a power which was seeking to reconcile and balance, to heal pains and close wounds. The Archangel seemed to offer unconditional gifts and wrap me up, like a small child in loving arms. Much of the healing energy seemed to come from the colours and I remembered later that the Violet Ray is regarded by esotericists as the healing ray. Modern healers use rose quartz and amethyst crystals to encourage healing; the colour of these stones will naturally vibrate with Raphael, so the healer has made contact with the Archangel's healing function when she uses the crystals.

The Kabbalist tradition links Raphael, rather than Gabriel, with Mercury. I am rather puzzled by this: Mercury is often depicted with a caduceus, which is a symbol of healing, and he is the patron saint of travellers, which fits part of Raphael's role in the Tobias story. But, as a personality, Mercury is usually seen as androgynous; he represents the mental processes, is a god of science and commerce and 'signifieth subtill men, ingenious, inconstant: rymers, poets, advocates, orators, phylosophers, arithmeticians, and busie fellowes' (Ben Jonson's masque *Mercury Vindicated*). This station of the tree is on the left pillar, described by the Kabbalist as passive, or feminine. My own feeling, after coming into intimate contact with this power, is that it has a feminine energy and, if we want to align it with one of the Olympians, would be connected to Aphrodite. Unlike her Roman counterpart Venus, with whom she is identified, Aphrodite was not only a deity of sexual love and beauty but also of affection and sociability. Certainly this energy would make a good travelling companion, would encourage a marriage and look for ways to reconcile and heal — Raphael performs all these functions in the story of Tobias. In the most famous Venusian myth the goddess is born from the foam of the sea where the penis of Uranus had fallen, following his emasculation by Saturn. We can see this as a healing myth, in which the foam of the ocean acts as an unction, soothing over a wound and creating something new and beautiful out of the old and discarded. In Homer, Aphrodite is the daughter of Zeus by his first wife, Dione. This would make her half-sister to Mercury (whose mother was Maia, daughter of Atlas); and it would seem reasonable to assume that some kind of working relationship between them was likely. She is a goddess of love, both human and spiritual, and is protectress of marriage and family life. For the astrologer, Venus is a highly aesthetic energy which seeks to manifest itself in some form of beauty and has an ennobling effect on human nature.

If we return to the Archangels with this mythological information in mind, we can understand that Raphael stands for a function which is conciliatory, healing, unselfish, harmonizing and inspirational. Raphael encourages unity and beauty: it promotes healing and transformation by shifting our consciousness towards relatedness and unconditional love. When the inspiration for this change has been encouraged by Raphael the activity has to be fired by Gabriel before the manifestation can take place in the kingdom. If we look at the birth of Jesus as a paradigm we could say that the conception takes place under the tutelage of Raphael, Gabriel brings the understanding of the process, participating in its capacity as messenger and interpreter of events, then the birth takes place under the guardianship of Sandalphon, who is identified with the Messiah in some Kabbalist literature. (In my own vision Sandalphon was accompanied by a lamb which is, of course, a conventional symbol for the Messiah).

Raphael is present where any desire emerges to make things good and beautiful: at a wedding; at the conception of a child; at a dance, at any kind of healing session including conventional surgery (Florence Nightingale is an example of a human living this archetype to the full); at religious gatherings; at any ceremony which joins humans in moving forward to create harmony.

The technique I was using for my inner journey meant that I was working back up an existing path whose original direction had been downwards. This means that I was arriving at each angelic door in reverse order: Raphael's function precedes that of Gabriel, whose function is to bring into awareness the processes from higher up the Tree, in order that they can be made manifest in the Kingdom. All the points above Gabriel are hidden from the intellect until we contact them via Gabriel. Raphael's function is secret, mysterious and unconscious; a hidden alchemy is being promoted. It takes Gabriel to bring the impetus into the conscious mind, and from thence into the light of day.

At this stage it is important to remember that there is a wide gap between the functions of the Archangels on the Tree of Life and the roles played by the mythological gods of Rome and Greece. The Archangel has been given a task in the creative process by a Divine Intelligence which knows what it wants to manifest and how to make it happen. The Archangel has a place in this process and is bound to abide within that framework. The only creature which has any choice in the acting out of Divine Will is the human being. In the Olympian myths the archetypes are depicted as gods and goddesses who are in a continual state of conflict, warring and competing with each other. Although there is a chief god, usually Jupiter but sometimes Apollo, the sun-god, he seems to have no abiding authority and, in any case, he is only one of the archetypes and is not a transcendent, creative power in his own right. We can see that in ancient Rome and Greece the archetypes were experienced as competitive processes, some of which worked together more harmoniously than others — there were marriages as well as patricides. For the Kabbalist, who is basically a mystic, the universe is derived from a singular Creative Power which allows duality for the sake of diversity. The Archangels are ten great spiritual beings whose duty is to manifest the ten powers of the Great name of God. In this cosmology the archetypes, or powers, are bound by the underlying order and the only thing that can inhibit the proper unfolding of the Divine Plan is the reluctance of humankind to participate. This participation requires a surrender of the individual ego to the Divine Process which is represented in the map of the Tree of Life. In this model the Archangels serve creation, including the human race; we have been offered glimpses and insights into the creative process in order to encourage us to become truly involved in it.

In order to meet any of the Archangels it is necessary to acknowledge our position at the foot of the tree before attempting an ascent. Having grounded ourselves at Sandalphon we can move upwards to contact Gabriel and then to the left and up to meet Raphael. At this point we have made contact with the divine power of healing; we can call on Raphael when we want to encourage harmony between people in conflict, when we wish to initiate healings of mind or body and when we seek protection against wicked spirits — and don't forget, whenever you are working towards unification and truth, towards raising your own consciousness, there will always be a negative energy trying to shift the balance in the other direction. Open a door to meet an angel and there is bound to be a demon hiding in the shadows of the portal.

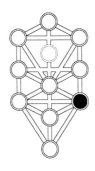

5

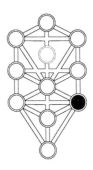

HANAEL

THE PROTECTOR

Tyger, tyger, burning bright
In the forests of the night,
What immortal hand or eye
Could frame thy fearful symmetry?

William Blake, *The Tyger*

After my exquisite encounter with Raphael I began to have doubts about the possibilities of progress. So far I had trusted my inner 'studio' to reveal the visions that I called for, but I had always had certain scriptural or traditional information to fall back on. I reassured myself that my original vision had been given uncalled for and that the content seemed to fit the text-book rather than the other way round. The next step after Hanael would be the famous Michael, so that was comforting. I had also had some glimpses of dwellers further up the tree, but Hanael was totally invisible to me until I had a sudden revelation one day, when I was doing some healing work.

Once I had discovered that Raphael was the Healer I had made it a habit to call on it when starting a healing session. I then decided to conduct an experiment: as the ten Sephiroth underly all manifestation we can use the Tree of Life as a model for the human body and look for the Sephiroth as power points, rather like chakras in the yogic system.

The process I used was to work with my hands on the etheric body, moving systematically over the whole body, calling on each Archangel as I arrived at the appropriate site on the client's body, asking it to help bring the body back into correct balance. At this stage I had only had intimate encounters with the lower three Archangels and some glimpses of a couple further up the tree.

On one occasion I was working on a client who suffered from ME and arrived at the area I thought should be covered by the Sephira Netzah, which is traditionally translated as Victory. I thought to myself that it was particularly important in this disease that the patient does not lose sight of the possibility of victory, that the fighting spirit should be encouraged and that quiet persistence and determination would win the day. I brought in the name of the Archangel Hanael and the vision came in with a rush — they usually do! As though they have been there all the time, behind a screen or curtain, and some mechanism has allowed a block to be cleared. Whenever I experience these sudden visions I am reminded of Blake's famous line, 'If the doors of perception were cleansed, everything would appear to man as it is, infinite.' I have the impression that the visions don't come to me. I go to them, but only when I have set up an appropriate occasion, when my mind is in the right space and my inner lens is clear.

My vision of Hanael was of a spinning cone of deep pink and cherry-red. The image was tall, beginning at a narrow base, circuiting out in brilliant, glowing coils into a wide disc which had shining spokes. This disc rotated in a persistent rhythm but changed angles, so that at one time I could only see the flat line of its edge and at another I could see it as a two dimensional mandala. From this disc rose another gyrating cone, much slimmer, which extended up and up into a fine line — I thought it resembled an arm holding up a sword. This creature was pure, vibrating, light with little suggestion of form; there was a shifting aura of fluttering pink which might have been feathers and a vague shapes at its extremities which reminded me of the changing outline of a Sufi dancer, a whirling dervish, who holds floating cloths which move up and down, up and across, as the dancer turns. The sound which accompanied it was like an intense droning with quite a high energy beat, like a drum, underlying it. The nearest thing I have heard to it is an Elizabethan dance called a branle or brawle, played on bagpipes, shawm and curtal, with a tabor beating the background. There was constant movement, tremendous energy and vitality, an unceasing, intense dynamic which was quite unnerving. I thought of the Red Queen in *Through the Looking-Glass* — always on the move, running to stand still. I had the feeling that this energy was so persistent, so demanding, that nothing would interrupt its flow. My favourite reference book told me that a better word for the function of the Sephiroth 'Netzah' than 'Victory' is 'Eternity', and this seemed entirely appropriate.

What floored me, once more, was the traditional planetary association: this Sephiroth, apparently, was linked with the planet Venus. My intuitive response to this energy is that it had more in common with Martian traits; the unceasing energy had a feel of positive assertion about it. Netzah, and therefore Hanael, is on the active side of the Tree and would be appropriate for the positive, masculine drive which astrologers attribute to Mars. The Martian archetype carries some difficulties for those of us who eschew war-like behaviour, directing ourselves towards Venusian co-operation and away from confrontation, and we may see him as only too physical, not at all arch-angelic! However, despite the soldier or warrior image that Mars carries, there is more this character than meets the eye.

The Greek version of Mars was Ares, and the philosophical Greeks regarded him as a braggart, bloodthirsty and brutal, even cowardly. He was a child of the incestuous relationship between Hera and Zeus and his brother was Hephaestos — Vulcan to the Romans — the lame smithgod. For the Romans Mars was a glorious soldier — we can see this splendid warrior archetype in the performance of Laurence Olivier in the wartime film of *Henry V*. But the golden armour is always a prelude to bloodletting:

The mailed Mars shall on his altar sit
Up to the ears in blood.

Henry IV Part One, IV.i

This was certainly the medieval view of Mars whose natives were seen as: 'theves and robbers... night walkers and quarell pykers, bosters, mockers and skoffers; and these men of Mars causeth warre, and murther, and batayle. They wyll be gladly smythes or workers of yron... lyers, gret swerers.'

In the myth concerning the birth of Mars we are told that he was conceived by Juno without a mate, having called upon Flora, goddess of flowering and blossoming plants who touched Juno on the head with a magical herb. Thus Mars was originally the Roman pastoral deity; he was patron of farmers and herdsmen and sometimes used the title 'Silvanus', meaning a dweller of the woods or forests. This role connects him with the Greek Pan, god of pastures, forests, flocks and herds, who also has a lustful nature and was a symbol of fecundity. The Vernal Equinox brings in the sign of Aries, ruled by Mars, and with it comes renewed growth and reproduction:

Universal Pan, Knit with the Graces and the Hours in dance,
Led on the eternal spring.

Milton, *Paradise Lost*, IV, 26

During March the Romans held a succession of festivals dedicated to Mars as God of War and as Protector of Growth. The sacred flame in the shrine of Vesta was re-lit on March 1st, and the priestly homes and sacred buildings were decorated with laurel. This plant was always associated with Mars and is still a symbol of victory and peace. The references we find to Mars and 'smythes and workers of yron', plus the connection with the pastoral life make me wonder whether Mars is not a conflation of the energies of the three Greek gods, Hephaestos, Pan and Ares. In Roman mythology Vulcan is the smith-god and is competitive with Mars over the possession of Venus (Aphrodite) — she was unfaithful to Vulcan and slept with Mars — and we get the impression that Mars takes over the role of being the natural male complement, and husband, to the female love energy of Venus. He is a macho figure, assertive, physically potent, sexually adventurous. If Raphael, the Healer, on the passive pillar of the Tree is our gentle, feminine principle of co-operation, sociability and caring, then Hanael, on the other, active Pillar, would be an opposite energy, with similar traits to Mars. If we develop the link between these images from the Greek and Roman myths and the vision that I encountered we can put together a picture of Hanael as an archetype which has a persistent, assertive drive towards creation and procreation; it underlies positive change and has a dynamic, unstoppable energy, able to resist negative and unnecessary change. It is Hanael who:

> *...fills the bed where lovers sleep,*
> *Male and female, damp armpits, moist legs.*
> *Stirs in the deep womb, fires the meeting cells,*
> *Stretches the white belly, fills the breast,*
> *Drives the infant in its journey to the air.*

All the assertive verbs I used in that stanza — 'stretches', 'fires', 'drives' — are appropriate for the energy which I met. This was why I chose Blake's Tyger poem to preface this chapter; every verse is filled with such verbs: 'aspire', 'seize', 'beat', 'clasp'; and the nouns: 'grasp', 'sinews', 'fire', give an impression of the ferocious intensity of the energy which I met in my vision and which Blake recognizes in the tiger. We, in our turn, need to address the same which the tiger provokes in Blake: can this energy, this 'fearful symmetry', be attributed to the very same creativity, the same Divine Intelligence, which made the lamb? Blake's philosophy was inclusive, for him energy was delight and all energy was attributed to a wonderful creative power; opposites are necessary dynamics in creation and we should not take sides, not see the oppositions as 'good' and 'bad'. I believe the answer to Blake's question is 'Yes'; the Tyger, however ferocious, however potentially dangerous from our point of view, is part of the creation, as authentic and valid as the loveable lamb. The Kabbalist would say yes, and so would Blake. But Blake's question highlights a deep-seated problem, our fear of a certain kind of energy and the difficulty we have in handling it sensibly. Where there is great light there is the potential for great darkness and all the Archangels have a demon hovering in the background, waiting for the unevolved soul to step out of line. The archetypes need to be in balance, otherwise at each stage there is the likelihood that we can become too enamoured of one particular energy over another. Hanael supplies a necessary drive, for self -protection, for reproduction, for energetic involvement in creation, but the demon waiting in the wings is definitely dressed in scarlet; here we can be tempted to the most famous of sins, lust, anger... even murder. The spirited Elizabethan dance called the 'brawle', which I mentioned earlier, gave its name to a fight: the very same energy which you need for that whirling, vivacious activity is driven by adrenalin, which rises dramatically in moments of sexual arousal and anger — both these states are necessary for the protection and continuation of creation. It is the driving, consistent and persistent force in Nature...

The force that through the green fuse drives the flower
Drives my green age; that blasts the roots of trees
Is my destroyer...

The force that drives the water through the rocks.
Drives my red blood;...

Dylan Thomas, *The force that through the green fuse drives the flower*

We can call on Hanael when we are beginning new tasks which require energetic input, when we are under any kind of threat, from illness or difficult circumstances or when others threaten us, physically or at a psychic level. Athletes, sportsmen and great dancers need Hanael, so do explorers and missionaries. It acts like a magnet between couples, arousing passion and desire. This same desire encourages the need to climb mountains; it is goal directed, achievement oriented. It brings a great sense of empowerment and capability, it fortifies the Will and creates an armour against negativity. You will find it in any kind of keep fit class, calm in yoga, vigorous in aerobics. Its bright colours may make Raphael's ethereal hues seem pallid but they are equal and complementary partners in the cosmic dance and neither should be courted to the exclusion of the other.

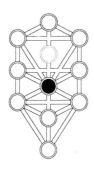

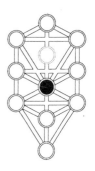

5

MICHAEL

THE LEADER

Angel, king of streaming morn;
Cherub, call'd by Heav'n to shine;
T'orient tread the waste forlorn;
Guide aetherial, power divine;
Thou, Lord of all within!

Golden spirit, lamp of day,
Host, that dips in blood the plain,
Bids the crimson'd mead be gay,
Bids the green blood burst the vein;
Thou, Lord of all within!

Soul, that wraps the globe in light;
Spirit, beckoning to arise;
Drives the frowning brow of night,
Glory bursting oe'r the skies;
Thou, Lord of all within!

Henry Rowe, *Sun*

It is said that the last words of the great painter Turner were 'The Sun is God'. Turner's genius for conveying the luminous in paint was born out of the new attitude to nature which developed in the romantic period, when the great poets transformed nature into a mystical substitute for religion. Rowe's poem 'The Sun' was written during this period and reiterates the Romantic intuition for the spiritual correspondence between man and nature: the Romantics asserted the value of individual experience and the Sun was seen as a metaphor for the primal power of the Self. Henry Rowe's poem speaks of the Sun as the 'power divine', 'the Lord within', and this coincides perfectly with the Kabbalist's understanding of

Michael as chief of the heavenly hosts, shining in golden armour. We can see an immaculate image of Michael in the brilliant statue which shines on the top of Mont St. Michel in France, his upheld arm brandishing the sword with which he is about to kill the dragon coiled at his feet, his head helmeted with a golden sunburst. On the Tree of Life model, Michael holds a central position marked by the Sefiroth 'Tiferet', translated as 'Beauty', which sits on the main axis of the Tree at the symmetrical centre, the point of equilibrium. Tiferet is poised halfway between Heaven and earth, partaking of both upper and lower worlds, where there is an exchange of the Divine with the material at the junction between the invisible and the visible. At this point on the Tree energies flow in from all directions and flow out again and we can understand it as the centralizing function in all organisms, all structures, whether abstract or concrete, and in human beings we call it the Self or the Soul. This function must take kingship and hold sovereign sway, acting as the focalizer for all the other functions, some of which have opposing drives and may, otherwise, challenge each other for supremacy. The name Michael translates as 'Like unto God', the Soul or Self is like God, and its source is God, but is not actually God, just as the Sun is not God — I hope Turner has now discovered his understandable error.

At this stage I want to make a small, but vital, diversion concerning gender. As far as I have any paltry glimpses of the nature of God I do not see that It can be defined in terms of gender. So in references to God, or Divine Intelligence or Creative Power, I always use the neutral pronoun. I mentioned earlier that the Archangels may seem to have masculine or feminine vibrations, perhaps 'yang' or 'yin' would be more useful as we do not necessarily associate these terms with human sexuality. On the left, passive pillar of the Tree of Life the energy is 'yin', or 'female', on the right 'yang' or 'male'. The Archangels on the central pillar can only be seen in terms of an energy which has no inclination either way; it is neutral as far as 'yin' or 'yang', 'male' or 'female' is concerned. Or we could see them as containing both energies in equal measure, thus they are seen as more potent, as turning points, as catalysts or as culminations. Michael, despite historical representation as a male figure, as soldier or Chief Warrior, stands on this central pillar and I shall refer to 'him' as 'it', just as I do with all the others. I am quite happy to use the term 'king' or 'lord' for such a being — I often refer to the Divine Intelligence as 'Lord' on the basis that a lord is someone to whom service and obedience are due. The fact that 'lords' and 'kings' have usually been male in the past is a peculiarity of the human race which, we are beginning to understand, is based on a lop-sided view of our own faculties.

During states of deep meditation I frequently find myself moving into a bright light, like brilliant sunshine, and I thought that I might well find Michael to have the same kind of light about it, that the meeting would be bright and that the Archangel would be a shining golden creature, much like the Mont St. Michel statue, though, hopefully, without male accoutrements. My thoughts were justified but I had underestimated quite how bright, how shiny, how potent, how awe-inspiring Michael is. The power has a presence about it which cuts one right down to size, and an energy which threatens to eliminate any human frailty, any meanness or small-mindedness.

When I used my corridor technique I found myself in complete darkness, black and velvety. Then the 'door' appeared, a magnificent portal, shining with bright colours, as though studded with magnificent jewels. I walked into an area which was like a vast hall, and although there was no solidity to the 'walls' they were luminous and transparent. I felt as though I was in a cathedral, or a building with a roof so high that it disappeared into the heavens. Light poured in through invisible windows and moved downwards in delicate rays and criss-cross shafts at quite a speed, like a laser show. There was a high singing sound which might have been one voice or a choir of thousands. There was no real melody, the notes hardly changed – I am no musician but I would say that they hovered around the top few notes of the scale of middle C. The Archangel itself beamed down from high up in the vaults of this ethereal building, its 'face' had just a suggestion of features, its 'wings' radiated like flashing rays of sunshine – 'gleaming feathers on molten, golden wings'. I was sitting in my usual chair at the time in 'that serene and blessed mood' which Wordsworth describes in his poem *Tintern Abbey* when:

> *...the breath of this corporeal frame*
> *And even the motion of our human blood*
> *Almost suspended, we are laid asleep*
> *In body, and become a living soul;*

otherwise I might well have fallen on my knees. Is this, I wondered, the angel of my dream poem and of my extraordinary encounter? Its presence was stunning, exhilarating, but not terrifying. There was a sense of immense power which challenged all doubt, all rationality, all ordinariness. But nonetheless I did not feel that its presence would 'overwhelm the mechanics of my brain', that my whole consciousness would be shifted into another dimension and that my everyday self would disappear into a cosmic hole. I felt safe, enriched, uplifted. I was at the edge of my own, usual world with a footing in another, which was not a separate reality but another layer, usually invisible. I wondered how much further I could go without losing everyday consciousness and with it the ability to recognize and report the experiences.

In Jungian psychology the self (the small 's' self) is understood to be moving towards a state of 'individuation' when full, individual maturity is reached. Post-Jungian astrologers understand the Sun as representing the Self, or essential nature, just as Kabbalists would describe Tiferet, personified as Michael, as representing the soul, the 'I am'-ness, the part of man which is truly in the image of God. Until this Archangel is recognized as lord, until the king takes up his sovereignship, we are unfulfilled, we are like an army marching with no one to issue orders, no one to map out the direction. Z'ev ben Shimon Halevi suggests that this is the meaning of the story of *Sleeping Beauty*: the real purpose of our lives is unrealized, dormant, until the prince carves through the tangles of our psychological forests and takes up residence in the palace of the soul. The animated film of *Sleeping Beauty* contained a ferocious and awesome dragon, which the prince had to slay in his quest for the princess. Michael is always depicted with a dragon at its feet: in the Book of Revelation Michael arrives, like a celestial Batman, to destroy a dragon with seven crowned heads and ten horns which is threatening the Virgin Mary and her Holy Child who has just been born. The dragon, or 'that great serpent', is understood to be Satan, the tempter who acted as the catalyst for the human race moving out of its state of innocence in the Garden. The dragon represents Doubt; it is Blake's 'Spectre', the figure which haunts us, always insinuating that we are only mortal beings, subject to time's laws, when we are, truly, celestial beings living in a material world whose laws bind us only while we are learning how to handle the responsibility of our divinity.

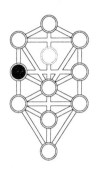

6

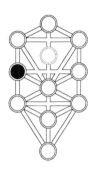

SAMAEL

THE ADMINISTRATOR

THE IMAGE
Water over lake: the image of LIMITATION.
Thus the superior man Creates number and measure,
And examines the nature of virtue and correct conduct.

A lake is something limited. Water is inexhaustible. A lake can only
contain a definite amount of the infinite quantity of water; this is its
peculiarity. In human life too the individual achieves significance through
discrimination and the setting of limits. Unlimited possibilities are not
suited to man; if they existed, his life would only dissolve in the boundless.
To become strong, a man's life needs the limitations ordained by duty and
voluntarily accepted.

I Ching: Hexagram 60 Chieh – Limitation

The next Archangel emerges from the Sephiroth Gevurah, translated as
'Judgement' or 'Strength'. Its name is Samael which translates as 'Poi-
soner' and it is known as the angel of evil. Previously its name was Lucifer,
bringer of Light, but this was changed after the fall from grace. This is
Satan, the tempter of the human race... so how does it come about that
we find the very devil occupying a place on the Tree of Life — especially
as we associate him with Death?

Both the Koran and the apocryphal *Book of Adam and Eve* relate the
fall of Satan (see Chapter One).When Adam and Eve were created, the
Divine Intelligence ordered all the angels and Archangels to bow down
and serve the new creatures. Satan declared that only God was worthy of
service and that he loved God too much to serve anyone else. For this sin
— of Pride — he was banished from the Divine Presence. After his fall he
hovers in the Garden of Eden in the form of the serpent, waiting to tempt
Adam and Eve out of their state of innocence.

I approached this character with understandable trepidation — one of my references had used the expression 'Cosmic Evil' in relation to it. I need not have worried. The vision was exquisite — although chilly! Having worked for some days with Michael's sunny nature I now found myself in the Arctic. I saw a stately woman, slender and very, very tall, in snowy drapes, sparkling with crystals. Behind the figure the sky was the palest blue and against this background radiated white patterns which seemed to grow and stretch from the head and shoulders of the figure, expanding into snowflake mandalas. All the movements were slow and graceful, as though in an action replay film. The features on the face were very clear cut, regal and with an exquisite serenity which bordered on severity. She wore a crown of immense height, seemingly made of crystal, carved with great precision into a three-storey palace with elaborate little turrets. This artefact added to the sense of grandeur and weight. She also carried a sword, very fine, like a fencer's rapier — it looked exceedingly sharp and precise. Her slow movements were accompanied by the sound of a bell, not a crisp, tinkling bell, as one might expect, but a gentle, almost muffled sound, on one note, persistent as the ticking of a loud clock.

I was very surprised that this archetype carried a female image; to me Satan had always been male. But the vessel of Gevurah is on the passive, or female, side of the tree. I felt I needed to work this one out. In the Judaeo-Christian tradition the female has had enough original sin piled on her, since the Creation myth tells us that it was Eve who first succumbed to temptation in the Garden. I thought of Andersen's Snow Queen who abducts little Kay and puts an icicle in his heart so that he cannot feel human emotion. I remembered the White Witch in Lewis' *The Lion, the Witch and the Wardrobe*, who tempts Edmund with Turkish Delight and promises of inheriting her kingdom. These ladies seem to echo the same archetype: they depict an aspect of creativity which appears to be rigid, unbending and extremely unfriendly. Why should it be seen as a female? Did these writers have particularly frigid mothers or is there an aspect of yin energy which is, by necessity, cool and therefore prone to freeze? During healing sessions I once came across this archetype wearing chain mail and on another occasion clothed entirely in steel grey armour. In both cases the vitality and sparkle which I saw in my vision were missing — the energy was very grey with little or no reflection. The pure archetype is very clear and clean, brilliant as snow on a sunny winter's day: there is a clarity and a precision which is quite attractive, though awe-inspiring.

Before taking the issue of the feminine quality of this energy further, it would seem appropriate to look at the myth from the point of view of human consciousness in general. Why is it that one of the Divine Attributes has to be cast out? I work on the assumption that Creation is under the ultimate control of the Creator, who has some outcome in mind and that nothing can actually happen to thwart the creative purpose. If there is Satan, an evil presence, then it is because God has permitted this situation.

The Satanic myth involves not only the fall of the Devil but also the fall of Man — Satan tempts Adam and Eve into separation from the Divine Garden, into a life which includes Death and pain. Part of the process of humanity is growth: the situation in the Garden was one of innocence, but it was also one of stasis. There was no evolving process. Being in the presence of God without knowing what it is like to be outside that presence, however briefly, is to have no knowledge at all. According to Mahomet, 'God was a hidden treasure, and desired to be known; so he created the world that He might be known.' An extension of that idea is to suggest that if you are born into a world of treasures you may not appreciate them until you have to do without! This concept suggests that God wants humanity to go on a treasure trail, a game of hide and seek. In order to do this there has to be some kind of drive, some mechanism which provokes the curiosity, a need to develop understanding. There has to be a spanner in the works.

At the point in the Creation myth where God tells the angels to bow down before Adam and Eve, the angels themselves must have some free will, otherwise Satan would not have had the opportunity to say 'No!'. Perhaps we should call Samael 'Cosmic No', rather than 'Cosmic Evil'. It is by saying 'No', that definition comes: all mothers will recall the two-year-old tantrums, when the little angel who had once been so amenable to mother's coaxing and persuasion develops into a little demon whose vocabulary seems to consists entirely of 'No!', 'Shan't!' and 'Don't want to!' This two-year-old is leaving the intimate union with its all-providing mother, a mystical oneness with its creator, and moving into self-awareness, learning how to define the self by refusing to be all-encompassing and accepting. Wise mothers understand this and do not believe that they are being rejected. As *I Ching* says, 'unlimited possibilities are not suited to man'; a wise mother also knows that the child must learn to accept 'No' when she uses the word herself.

We can see that in order for there to be diversity there has to be definition and that an organizing and separating process is vital for this to take place. In order to meet the Divine and know the Divine we must first have a separate identity; this identity has necessary pain attached to it, the pain of separation, but this same anguish is the grit in the oyster — it drives us, inexorably, to seek union with the One. Manifestation cannot take place without the creation of opposites; diversity requires the knowledge of 'this not that', there is no self-awareness without the shadow of not-self.

In the Old Testament the name Satan simply means 'adversary', and in the story of Job we find God allowing Satan to deprive Job of everything he owns and to cause him physical suffering. Here is 'a perfect and upright man', someone who has known the comforting aspect of God as Cosmic Yes, being brought to sharp and painful awareness of Cosmic No, for no apparent reason. It is because of our inability to fathom the reasons behind crisis and disaster that we have come to think of these lessons as a manifestations of 'bad luck' or of 'the devil's work'. We must remember though, that God gives Satan permission to test Job — Satan does not have the freedom to work in this way without reference to the overall Creative intention. It is not until much later stories that Satan develops into the spirit of Evil. Jewish philosophy is essentially monotheistic and the Kabbala provides a model of a creation which contains diversity and a variety of energies which interact and pull against each other but no basic dichotomy. The Tree of Life, with its three pillars, demonstrates how apparently opposing energies can work together in an harmonious unit.

After the Babylonian Exile the Jews were influenced by Persian dualism in which the concept of two conflicting principles, constantly warring for supremacy, developed. In Zoroaster's theology, dated at around the sixth century BC, the principle of light, Ahura Mazda, is opposed by Ahriman, the destructive spirit whose chief weapon is the demonic Az, a female principle who represents sexual and other desires, but also Doubt which weakens the intellect. By the time he appears in the apocryphal *Book of Enoch*, written after the second century BC, the Devil has crystallized into the form we recognize today. The Christian Gnostic sects developed a very precise dualism: they saw two separate worlds and the Devil became a lord in his own right, the 'demiurge', who ruled the material world, which was seen as fallen and irredeemable. In this philosophy our archangel has become a threat to creation rather than a necessary mechanism within it.

Having explored the role of the Archangel Samael, aka Satan, aka Lucifer, as a separating principle and seen it, hopefully, in a more positive light, we need to return to the question of feminine energy and its relationship with a principle which human beings tend to identify as negative, threatening and dark. As we have seen, Persian mythology associated the feminine principle with darkness and evil. In early Christian Gnostic mythology the Devil was in league with the female principle who is 'without foreknowledge, wrathful, double-minded, double-bodied, a virgin above and a viper below'. Medieval artists often depicted the tempter as half-female, half-snake, coiled up the Tree of Knowledge in the Garden of Eden. Western thinking is still stuck with this vision of a world in which negative archetypes are at work, always threatening to destroy us and the things we create. But we need to take a more holistic view. The material world is subject to flux and change and the cyclical processes of birth and death; this can be seen as feminine since the female of the species is also subject to flux and change and participates intimately in the birth process. It is worth noting that the word 'material' has the same etymological root as 'mater', or 'mother'. Dualistic thinking tends to see the physical body as a prison in which spirit is trapped, and the generative and degenerative cycles as a threat to the spirit. Even so-called 'rational' philosophers like Descartes, understood themselves as being a combination of two very different substances —spirit (or mind), and body (or matter). Descartes floundered in his attempts to fathom how these two substances were united in a single human being or in creation generally, but out of this 'Enlightened' philosophy grew the mechanistic worldview which science has taken on board, a view in which the natural world is seen as something which is to be measured and controlled. If Descartes had emerged from his cogitations with a unifying, rather than a divisive philosophy, Western society might have paid due respect to Nature rather than engaging in the rape and pillage of its Mother. Spinoza, a Jewish philosopher, brought a monotheistic perspective to the problem; he rejected the Cartesian dualism and saw only 'one infinite substance, of which finite existences are modes or limitations.' Thus Spinoza denied any transcendent distinction between good and evil; for him the Divine Intelligence was immanent in all creation. It seems unfortunate that Western thinking has followed the Cartesian lead; it might have been healthier to have taken up the more holistic philosophy of Spinoza in which Nature is seen with a Wordsworthian eye:

> *And I have felt*
> *A presence that disturbs me with the joy*
> *Of elevated thoughts: a sense sublime*
> *Of something far more deeply interfused,*
> *Whose dwelling is the light of setting suns,*
> *And the round ocean and the living air,*
> *And the blue sky, and in the mind of man:*
> *A motion and a spirit, that impels*
> *All thinking things, all objects of all thought,*
> *And rolls through all things.*

William Wordsworth, *Tintern Abbey*

The ecological crisis we find ourselves in has emerged from a fundamental mistake in our thinking, which has rejected the material, the feminine principle, naming it evil and casting it into the shadows. The Kabbalist's model demonstrates that this principle is an essential function of the whole, even if its energy initiates events, such as the death of the body, which we find threatening.

So far we have explored the myth of this archetype in its role as a principle which divides and separates in order to create new possibilities. There is another key issue involved: in order to have a creative process in which things grow and change, fall away and permit fresh things to be manifested, we must live in a world of Time. In Greek myth Time is represented by the god Kronos, Saturn to the Romans. Kronos emasculated his own father Ouranos, the sky god, in order to separate him from perpetual sexual intercourse with the earth goddess, Gaia. This perpetual love making meant that Gaia could not give birth to her children. Here we have an echo of the Garden of Eden; potential and creative wealth cannot be brought to fruition without some other principle interfering and, apparently, upsetting the apple cart. In this case the stasis is interrupted by Time for without it Gaia cannot give birth. In this myth Kronos seizes control of the world in much the same way as the Demiurge becomes ruler of the fallen world in the Gnostic myth. But this is necessarily so; without Time the world does not exist.

The familiar images of Saturn as Old Father Time, especially in his skeletal form when portrayed as the Grim Reaper with the sickle, are reminders of the processes of life and death and the darkness and shadows which we fear. The names Saturn and Satan are, not coincidentally I suggest, very similar. In astrological symbolism Saturn represents structure and form, government and justice. It is the principle which crystallizes undifferentiated energy into the manifest universe. He is sometimes called 'Lord of the Boundaries', and represents limitation. *I Ching* uses images of water and the limiting lake; another useful image is that of molten gold, representing divine energy, which has to be poured into moulds in order to set and become tangible treasure. Gold was often poured into shapes made of sand which could be swept away after the gold had solidified. This provides a useful metaphor; the structures have to be there but they do not need to be permanent or rigid. My vision was clad in snow flakes. They are elaborate structures which are subject to rapid dissolution, they melt and reform, each time creating fresh patterns, every one unique. In *The Snow Queen* Kay, the little boy with the icicle in his heart, had to spell out the word 'Eternity' before he could be set free; Eternity is beyond the structures of time and the manifest world and if we remember this we will no longer be in fear of the processes of change or of death.

There is an old saying, 'Give the Devil his due', and I take this to mean that even the archetype of Time, which seems so destructive, has to be recognized and given respect. Every process in which we participate, whether it is a creative endeavour with a tangible end-product, such as baking a cake or making a dress, or an intellectual or social endeavour involving writing a book or setting up an organization, are all subject to the laws of Time. How Time works for us — I emphasize 'for' — depends on our attitude to it, and our attitude will, in turn, depend on our understanding of the processes which the soul has to engage in on its journey back to the One. We need to honour Samael and give it permission to take its place among the other archangels — as long as it agrees that its place is just one role on a tree growing towards unification.

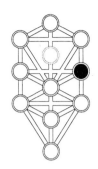

7

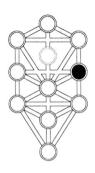

ZADKIEL

THE COMFORTER

The Lord is my shepherd, I shall not want. He maketh me to lie down in green pastures: he leadeth me beside the still waters.

He restoreth my soul: he leadeth me in the paths of righteousness for his name's sake. Yea, though I walk through the valley of the shadow of death, I will fear no evil: for thou art with me; thy rod and thy staff they comfort me.

Thou preparest a table before me in the presence of mine enemies; thou anointest my head with oil; my cup runneth over. Surely goodness and mercy shall follow me all the days of my life: and I will dwell in the house of the LORD for ever.

Psalm 23

Once we have come to terms with the limitations of Samael and taken them seriously but lightly, as sand or snowflakes, we can move across to the right side of the tree, to the Sephiroth Hesed, or Mercy, where sits the Archangel Zadkiel. In *The Lion, the Witch and the Wardrobe* one character, speaking about the White Witch, declares that while she rules 'it is always winter and never Christmas'. If Samael is a Snow Queen, crystallizing energy into manifestation, then Zadkiel is Father Christmas, bringing of gifts of joy and the experience of knowing the Eternity which Kay needed to spell out.

In order to meet with Zadkiel we need to recognize that limitations only exist in order to make things happen in the temporal world and that time itself is an artefact which we are co-creating. When this is experienced we are filled with the certainty that, as Julian of Norwich said, 'All will be well and all manner of things will be well'. The author of the 23rd Psalm knew it too.

My experience when I set off to call on Zadkiel was very much one of breaking through a barrier and suddenly feeling I had no sense of solidity or groundedness. I had half expected to meet a St. Nicholas-style bishop, dressed in ecclesiastical reds and golds, probably enthroned in a glorious building. But I had left buildings behind. After I left Samael I could not even find a corridor; I was quite in the dark, although the dark was soft and cosy with no sense of threat. I began to grope and found myself pressing on velvety walls on all sides. I seemed to be in a very gentle prison. I kept trying, methodically proceeding around the walls like a blind man trying to find a door. Predictably, it was when I gave up that the answer came. Quite suddenly a bright white space appeared, like a film screen with only white light shining on it. I wasn't sure whether it was solid or not; I stretched out a hand and found myself sliding through it, like Alice through the looking glass. When I emerged on the other side I felt as though I had been fragmented and then put back together in a rather unusual way. I kept looking at myself to see if all my bits were there. All my limbs seemed intact but they were peculiarly shiny and my clothes seemed to have a bright glaze on them.

There was a great noise around me, like a symphony orchestra playing triumphant music. I kept thinking I could identify the music, that it might be 'Jerusalem', or 'Land of Hope and Glory', or some other patriotic piece; it wasn't quite any of those but nonetheless conveyed the same kind of power and emotion.

I became aware that I could not identify my whereabouts, that I was, apparently, suspended in a deep space. I could feel no solidity around me or under my feet, everything was bright and white — as though I had walked into the reverse situation from the dark enclosure where I had been a few moments before. The music was majestic and seemed to come from all directions; I was surrounded by invisible musicians. I began to think of the lines of a hymn: 'in light inaccessible hid from our eyes'. Had I arrived at an aspect of the Divine which was so formless that I would not see anything at all?

The bright whiteness began to vibrate into patterns which I can only describe as curls and I began to shake slightly. The curls rolled all around me, ebbing and flowing like waves. I wanted them to be a curly white beard and long flowing locks, but there was no face that I could find. I was at a loss; I felt I was in the presence of some enormous power, I felt quite safe but wondered what I could do or say to make some communication. Then it came to me: ' I think you are wonderful!' The curly patterns whirled into a tornado and I was seized in to it, then I found myself falling through a tunnel of a deep blue-purple colour, almost fluorescent, a glowing, smooth and sensuous colour. I fell through soft folds of this wonderful mauve — almost like a silky-satin to the touch — until I made a gentle landing on a cushiony floor, where I lay in a stupor for a few minutes before I brought myself out my meditation and back to my own room. Phew! Who needs a fun park?!

When I had gathered my thoughts together I began to write down my impressions of the encounter; there was not much to say from the visual point of view, but I wanted to get to grips with my psychological responses. The most important thing was that I had felt I was perfectly safe despite the fact that I had no idea what, if anything, was holding me up. In cartoons the characters sometimes go on walking in mid-air when a steel girder has been removed, and when they notice it has gone they plummet. I noticed there was nothing obviously supporting me but I had no sense of panic; I stayed put. There had been a sense of cosiness and comfort about the whole adventure, right from the start — even in the velvety cell I had not felt trapped or claustrophobic, just protected. The feeling that I had been in contact with a power which was comforting and caring continued for some hours, and now I only have to close my eyes for a moment to recall it and find perfect reassurance. When I consulted my Kabbalist I found that the Sephiroth Hesed is associated with the planet Jupiter. For once I found this suggestion extremely appropriate, from the astrologer's point of view. 'This is the point of expansion, of great energy before it is checked by Gevura. Also attributed to this Sephiroth are the qualities of magnificence, magnanimity, mercy, all marks of Jupiter the beneficent god.' (Z'ev ben Shimon Halevi, *Tree of Life.*) I felt this matched the energy of the Archangel I had met. The planet Jupiter is an extraordinarily large cosmic body, so large, and with such a low mean density, that it is almost a star — its outer layers are gaseous although it probably has a solid core. It has twelve moons of its own and seems to be the centre of its own system. In Greek mythology, Zeus, the equivalent of the Roman Jupiter, or Jove, was the greatest of the Olympians, a God among gods. In psychological astrology he represents expansion and enthusiasm which, without the use of judgement — Saturn — can bubble over and be wasted; uncontrolled expansion is extremely dangerous. Another name for the Sephiroth Hesed is Gedulah — Greatness. There is dynamic here for tremendous creativity but without discipline it may be so much hot air, or lead to a total disregard for duty and responsibility. Zeus and his Latin counterpart, Jupiter, were both known for their profligate behaviour and the numerous offspring from their excesses.

We have seen how Raphael and Hanael make a couple, one yin the other yang, on their respective pillars, each providing an opposite but complementary energy. In the same way Samael and Zadkiel are a pair, the one limiting and stern, the other encouraging and merciful. One inhabits the Valley of the Shadow of Death, the other provides the green pastures and the cup of oil; the first we avoid, the second we seek. We could see this pair as a Puritan and a Cavalier and recognize that both types are a pain when they get carried away with their own line of thought.

The Puritans were originally a group of English Protestants who wanted to 'purify' the ceremonies of the church, abolishing any forms which were not based on scripture. The wanted to strip away the fancy bits and get back to the essence of Christianity. Very laudable; but in their zeal they created a strait jacket for themselves, trampling on creativity and sponsoring the dreaded work ethic, based on guilt. Nowadays school children asked about Oliver Cromwell only know that 'he was against fun, wasn't he?'

The Cavaliers were Roman Catholic; this Church had become extremely lax in its spiritual life until it was challenged by people like Luther, when it started to clean up its act. Nowadays we use the word 'cavalier' to mean 'free and easy' or 'offhand'. It is the tension and potential conflict between two apparently opposing energies that means we have to have a commanding officer in the form of Michael. In Shakespeare's play *Twelfth Night* we come across these two in the characters of Malvolio and Sir Toby Belch. Malvolio's name means 'evil wisher' and seems to be a direct reference to Saturn — the medieval astrologers thought Saturn to be 'malefic'. He is the puritan and kill-joy, seeking to squash the exuberance of Sir Toby and his merry-making buddies. He is po-faced and pretentious and the others gang up on him, seeking to ridicule him and contrive to have him locked up. At that point Feste, the clown, takes advantage of Malvolio's wretched position and derides him. Then we see the strength and dignity which Malvolio can muster; his sense of propriety gains the upper hand and we, the audience, find ourselves sympathizing with him. The twelve nights of Christmas have always been an excuse for excessive behaviour, of relinquishing all usual responsibilities and dropping the daily formalities of life. The office party provides a good example of a modern Saturnalia. Shakespeare's message is that it is all very well breaking all the boundaries of good taste and self-restraint but there has to be a limit, and if that limit is broken there will be karmic repercussions — in the second act, Feste says that 'pleasure will be paid, one time or another', and Malvolio's parting shot is ' I will be revenged on the whole pack of you.'

Zadkiel's energy is present when there is boundless energy and enthusiasm for a new task or where there is hope in the process of life, even in the presence of death. It is very helpful to call on the Archangel when someone is grieving or in shock — often, of course, he makes its presence felt without anyone deliberately calling him. The Archangels are always present and always functioning, but to a great extent we have lost touch with their process and only become aware of them at points of crisis. If you are working on a new enterprise which will demand a lot of initial optimism and faith then Zadkiel needs to be reminded of your intentions — but remember to call up the necessary controlling energy of Samael as well, otherwise you may overspend your budget. There have been suggestions, mainly by astrologers, that Jupiter can be identified with Yahweh or Jehovah of the Old Testament: this equation seems to be based on the roles of Jupiter in Roman myth such as 'imperator' — supreme commander; Tonans — thunderer, 'Invictus' — invincible and 'Triumphator' — 'triumphant'. Jupiter was the special protector of the Romans as Yahweh was for the Hebrews. We can also recognize the comforting aspect of God in the 23rd Psalm as the archetype of Jupiter in astrology, both modern and traditional. The Archangel Zadkiel is the last of 'the seven spirits before the throne', and his energy is beyond the limitation of Samael, but there are more Archangels to come. When we burst through the boundaries and meet the potency of Zadkiel it may be tempting to think we have arrived, that we know God, but seven steps only take us to the outskirts of heaven, not through the gateway.

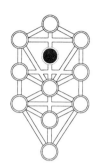

INTERLUDE
THE HOLY SPIRIT

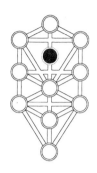

If we continue to ascend the Tree of Life we next arrive at the most mysterious junction, Daat, described as a 'non-Sefirah' which is unmanifest but has 'a place within manifestation'. It acts as a veil between the seven lower Sefiroth and the three so-called 'supernal' Sefiroth; 'supernal' means belonging to a higher realm, usually heaven — that is, divine. We have already come across Raphael's reference to the 'seven spirits before the throne'; now we have come to an invisible threshold where there is no Archangel, no point of communication.

In order to reach further into heaven, into the celestial citadel itself, we have to surrender our sense of personal being and melt into No-thing. This experience will be familiar to people who practice meditation — it is known as 'transcending'. In mystical literature this space is called 'The Cloud of Unknowing', 'The Abyss of the Godhead', 'Nirvana' — the ego dies and there is the experience of self-annihilation, a stripping away of personal self-hood, knowledge and time, all of which is replaced by a sense of fulfilment, of coming home.

In Elizabethan literature the loss of self in sexual orgasm is called *la petit mort*, 'the little death' — the lover forgets herself in the beloved — and the mystical death has much in common with this experience. The physical sensations, such as tingling and trembling, which are associated with it are so close to the erotic sensations experienced in love-making that it is no surprise to those familiar with both mystical and sexual surrender to find erotic metaphors in writings such as *The Song of Solomon* and the testament of Teresa of Avila. The Prophet Mahomet said 'you have to die before you die', meaning that we have to surrender the ego conscientiously, during our lifetime, before we can die a fully conscious death when it is time to relinquish the material body.

Traditional pictures of the Tree of Life often depict it as a tree with its roots in the air and its top branches under the earth. In this representation the three supernal Sefiroth are seen in the roots and Malkut, the Kingdom, is at the top of the tree. This is a visual reminder that the Crown of the Tree and the Root of the Tree are one and that the Kingdom is not only descended from the Crown but supported by it, as the growth of the tree is fed and nourished by its roots. The heavenly three, centred on Kether, are both the rulers and the servants of the Kingdom and its courtiers. There is an alchemical marriage, in which Kether acts as the groom to the bride of Malkut and Daat is the veil that necessarily separates them; when they are united there is no manifestation, because there is no separation — just as in the myth of Uranus and Gaia there could be no children while they were in a constant state of physical union.

The Kabbalist refers to Daat, the 'non-Sefirah', as 'Ruah ha Kodesh', the Holy Spirit, and states that it is the point at which the Absolute may enter at will to intervene directly in existence. Daat is translated as 'Knowledge', a place of certainty which emerges from the Sefiroth Binah — Understanding, and Hokhmah — Wisdom. Psychologically it is a place of resolution, where speaks 'the still, small voice of calm', of certain knowledge. We can encourage the strength of this certainty by regular meditation. The Maharishi, who teaches Transcendental Meditation, uses the analogy of dipping a cloth into a dye and, in the Indian tradition, laying it out in the sun to dry. The drying process, which reduces the depth of colour, represents our daily contact with the ordinary world in which our sense of certainty may be regularly undermined. Constant re-dipping of the cloth builds up the colour over a period of time, until the colour reaches its full strength. In the same way, regular excursions into the Divine Abyss, in which we experience our own annihilation at a personal level, increases our contact with the underlying Reality of the true Self which can then act from a state of real Knowledge. True, unconditional surrender to this Knowledge is painful and frightening: many people who take up meditation practices are prepared to do so on the basis that their lives will be improved at a material level. It is the case that meditation will improve the quality of life and usually the benefits are noticed quite quickly, but there may be a rocky ride if there are any underlying resistances, or if the will is only prepared to relinquish a part of its own control. Taking a step into Daat involves trusting the abyss, putting out a hand without seeing that there may be a hand to receive you, walking a tightrope without a safety net.

Angels of Extinction

Come, spirits, with your flaming wings,
Seep through the confines of my face
And let me hear what heaven sings.
Enter in this most secret place,
Slide through my skin and bone
Into the dark recesses of my skull,

Where I am and I alone.
Then all my thoughts make null
And with your burning gyres
Annihilate my self-will and my desires.

Daat represents a point of exchange between the trinity of supernal Sefiroth, the trinity of the Godhead in Christian terminology, and the concrete world: it is that narrow margin between the outstretched finger of God and the outstretched finger of Adam which we see in Michelangelo's portrayal of the creation of humanity on the Sistine Chapel ceiling. The energy which crosses that gap is the Holy Spirit — it energizes Adam from being simply a creature of clay into a living being:

And the LORD God formed man of the dust of the ground, and breathed into his nostrils the breath of life; and man became a living soul.

Genesis 2:7

With this breath, we inherit not simply the mechanism by which we breathe, but an innate knowledge of our Divine origin, of our direct link with the Creative Intelligence. Frequent visits to this no-space will remind us constantly of our Divine inheritance and will stimulate us to move gradually closer to living in accordance with the original intention of our own individual Self — this may mean dramatic shifts away from the social intentions or the aims of our inheritance, which can lead to painful re-orientation in life-style, until we are back on our true course. D.H. Lawrence recognized the power of the Godhead to re-direct the psyche in this extract from his poem, *Shadows:*

And if in the changing phases of man's life
I fall in sickness and in misery
my wrists seem broken and my heart seems dead
and strength is gone, and my life
is only the leavings of a life...
then I must know that I am still in the hands of the unknown God,
he is breaking me down to his own oblivion
to send me forth on a new morning, a new man.

D. H. Lawrence, *Shadows*

Much of Lawrence's work indicates that he was a natural mystic, but we might speculate that if he had been able to reach into Daat on a regular basis, using one of the meditation techniques that have been opened up to us since his death, he might not have felt so traumatized by occasions of 'sickness' and 'misery'. People who are able to get in touch with, or have brief glimpses of, the Knowledge in their own psyche, find it easier to accept the 'slings and arrows of outrageous fortune', seeing them as a working out of a necessary process of personal evolution. Gradually, the regular contact with Knowledge will increase access to Wisdom and Understanding (Binah and Hokhmah) and the vicissitudes of life will become less extreme: our soul ships will settle on a gentle ocean, rather than be tossed on one which is choppy, or wild. Real Knowledge will enable us to take charge of the voyage: 'You are the Captain of your ship and the Master of your Soul' was frequently quoted to me as a child. Captaincy is Michael's task but in order to be a Captain Michael needs Knowledge — it needs a map and the navigational knowledge necessary to use it.

There is no Archangel assigned to this point on the Tree of Life: the Kabbalist is saying that it has a place in manifestation, but is not manifest; it is an interface between the upper and lower parts of the tree. If we wanted to look for an astrological indicator for this point I would suggest that Chiron fits the bill.

Chiron is the name for an unusual body which was first identified by astronomers on November 1st 1977. Its peculiarity lies in the fact that it is larger than an asteroid yet rather small to be a planet, and that it has an erratic orbit. Mathematical models which have successfully predicted the positions of planets (e.g. Bode's Law) make no allowances for the position of another where Chiron was found. Astronomers have coined the word 'planetoid' in an attempt to classify Chiron, but it has also been suggested that Chiron is a comet which has stopped for a visit, rather than just passing through. Chiron was discovered between Saturn, last of the seven traditional planets, visible to man with the naked eye, and Uranus, first of the outer planets, only observable since we have created advanced telescopes. Its elliptical orbit seems to create a link between these two planets, which are seen as personal on the one hand and transpersonal on the other. This makes Chiron an ideal candidate for an archetype representing Daat. Melanie Reinhart in her book, *Chiron and the Healing Journey*, suggests that the theme of maverick, outsider or loner is appropriate for Chiron — Daat is the only non-manifest point on the Tree of Life, and thus is an oddity, like Chiron.

If we look at the points on the Tree with our astrological eye we can understand the seven Archangels on the lower branches as representative of the seven 'personal' planets of traditional astrology. The three further planets, discovered since humanity began to look beyond life on home territory, are indicators of 'transpersonal' energies in the psyche; these three can be equated with the three supernal Archangels. Chiron can be seen as acting as a go-between, linking the inner and the outer, bridging the gap between the divine and the material. The mythological Chiron was a centaur, half man and half horse — a suitable duality for our purposes, since the upper half is man, potentially wise and intelligent, and the lower half is animal, instinctual and energetic. Chiron was the wisest of the centaurs and taught the Greek heroes healing, music and hunting. Modern astrologers are still grappling with the concept of Chiron as an archetype but a picture is beginning to emerge, particularly encouraged by Melanie Reinhart's perceptive book. Melanie suggests that the myth of Chiron encourages astrologers to think of his role in the natal chart as that of the wounded healer. In the original Greek tale, Chiron's own healing abilities were not sufficient to heal his own wound, received in a brawl started by other, less evolved, centaurs who were fighting with the hero Hercules. The wound, from a poisoned arrow, provoked Chiron to search for a cure: his mission enabled him to increase his own healing abilities, even though he was unable to heal himself. Being immortal, Chiron could not die from his wound and his eventual release came when he offered to change place with Prometheus, bound to a rock by Zeus (the Greek version of Jupiter) for stealing the fire of the gods. The fire represents a higher state of consciousness and the power that accompanies it. Each day Prometheus suffered his liver being plucked out by a griffin, and the liver was renewed each night by Zeus in order that the torment could be endlessly re-enacted. Zeus agreed that Prometheus could be released if an immortal would take his place and relinquish his own immortality. Chiron's case was pleaded by Hercules and the centaur took the place of Prometheus. Eventually Chiron died and was given back his immortality as the constellation Centaurus and the griffin was slain by Hercules. This myth provokes an image of a healer/saviour in the tradition of Jesus Christ; the binding on the rock is an echo of the surrender by Jesus on the tree, but also of other myths in which enlightenment only comes after torment which involves being painfully bound to the material world.

For modern astrologers, then, Chiron symbolizes the wound and the potential it brings for healing. Does the myth of Chiron add to our understanding of the role of Daat — The Holy Spirit? The connecting role Chiron plays in the solar system, when used as a model for the functioning of the psyche, seems appropriate, as we see him making a bridge between the personal and the transpersonal. So does the duality of Chiron, part wise human, part intelligent animal; the upper and lower branches of the Tree are linked by a maverick — a 'non-Sefirah'. What about the wounding and the healing?

We can use Chiron as model for the human attempt to reconcile the apparently opposing needs of spirit and matter in its own being: in Chiron this conflict is reconciled in his own centaur body and in the harmony he brings to the lives of the heroes, through his teaching. When he becomes wounded he represents the pain which we all feel when we recognize our own divine nature and start struggling towards creating a true balance between body and soul. In Michelangelo's painting of God giving life to Adam, we see humanity receiving a very questionable gift — it is the gift of self-knowledge. All the other creatures have been given the breath of life, but no Divine Breath, self-knowledge. This gift carries a painful responsibility.

In one version of the myth, Chiron's wound is received after he goes to a party, in another when he becomes involved in a battle following a rape by another centaur. In both versions we see him reduced to a merely social creature, abandoning his true role as wise teacher. If we behave as social beings and put our divine inheritance on the back boiler we, also, are liable to be wounded by the arrows of a divine principle which urges us on to discover our own cosmic nature and live correctly. If we accept a link between the three supernal Sephiroth and the three outer planets it may be of significance that two of the three were in 'wounding' signs of the Zodiac when Chiron was discovered: Neptune in Scorpio and Uranus in Sagittarius. (Scorpio provides the poison for the arrow of Sagittarius.) Since the arrival of Chiron we have become increasingly aware that our social habits have put our own bodies and that of our Mother, the Earth, at risk; we have recognized the wound and have started to search for a cure.

Melanie Reinhart debates the connection to Chiron of the myth of Prometheus, who was punished for stealing fire from Zeus. If Zeus/Jupiter has an archetype which resonates with Zadkiel, the comforter, the last of the seven archangels 'before the throne', then we can understand that we are taking a risk if we attempt to encroach further up the tree without sanction, taking that which is not given. Prometheus stretched up in heaven without the necessary surrender at the threshold and his pain can only be solved by some kind of grace. Melanie suggests that Prometheus, connected with the sign of Aquarius by some astrologers, may be a guiding spirit for our age, representing

> *the clear recognition of the need to uphold our human values whatever the cost, and a parallel warning to give the gods their due. He represents the struggle of individuality emerging from enchainment by the forces of oppression which do not value human life...*

It is the Knowledge of the Holy Spirit, received at Daat, which strengthens the purpose and directs Michael, the inner Leader at Tiferet; this struggle can then unfold purposefully but wisely and with the minimum of conflict. The struggle has to work with the unfolding processes of the collective and with the proper potential of the human race always in mind, otherwise our attempts to provoke political change will simply be another attempt to steal fire. Prometheus, we might also note, was reputed to have made humanity out of clay and water, it is a goddess, Athene, who breathes life into the creature, but this part of his story nonetheless resonates with the concept of the Holy Spirit, which is the necessary ingredient to raise humanity to consciousness.

We have inherited the myth of Prometheus in the form of a play by Aeschylus, *Prometheus Bound*, in which Zeus behaves as a crude tyrant, and Prometheus, although not presented as a blameless victim, heroically resists all the mental and physical tortures which are heaped upon him in an attempt to break his will. Eventually a reconciliation is effected between them. The Romantic poet Shelley, writing in the early nineteenth century, was offended by what he saw as a moral compromise between Prometheus and Jupiter: 'I was averse from a catastrophe so feeble as reconciling the Champion with the Oppressor of mankind.'

My own approach to the archetypes does not encompass labelling one of them as 'oppressive', but it is not at all difficult to see in the Archangel Zadkiel a patriarchal archetype which does not actively encourage further spiritual development. After all, if we arrive in the safe arms of a comforter who leads us in pastures green, makes us to lie down and fills our cup to overflowing, why go any further on our journey? Shelley called his own version of the story *Prometheus Unbound* and concentrated on the mental struggle between Prometheus and Zeus/Jupiter rather than on the external brutality. In Shelley's play it becomes clear that Prometheus, by cursing Jupiter, has locked himself into a vicious cycle with the very energy which he seeks to undermine. This is essentially a masculine struggle, a conflict of two mighty and uncompromising wills. Then Shelley introduces the redeeming role of love in the feminine character of Asia who is guided by dreams and intuition. Asia undergoes a spiritual rebirth — a chariot arrives 'inlaid with crimson fire' guided by a young spirit 'with dove-like eyes of hope', and invites her to ascend. The fire and the dove are standard symbols for the presence of the Holy Spirit and its grace, and we can see in Shelley's version of the story a fresh approach to the question of union and transcendence. He has introduced an essential ingredient missing from the Greek, the intuitive processes of the feminine.

If we understand the myth-making and poetic imagination of humanity to be accessing the depths of consciousness in which lie the answers to the human condition, we can find powerful messages in the Greek tales and the poetry of Shelley. It is not without significance that when Shelley was writing *Prometheus Unbound* two of our 'supernal' planets were in conjunction — as they are at present. At that time Uranus and Neptune were in the sign of Sagittarius — a fire sign which fires arrows and is said to be ruled by Chiron. Shelley was born in 1792, very much a child of the revolutionary period which had been ushered in with the discovery of the first of the outer three planets, Uranus, in 1781. He was only too conscious of the changes that were in the ether; in a letter defending himself against imitation he pointed out that great poets derive 'from the new springs of thought and feeling, which the great events of our age have exposed to view, a similar tone of sentiment, imagery and expression. A certain similarity all the best writers of any particular age inevitably are marked with, from the spirit of that age acting on all.'

If, as Melanie Reinhart suggests, Prometheus himself is a hero for our own age, representing the Aquarian urge to break the chains of our spiritual limitations, then I feel we should recognize Shelley's powerful insights into the human condition and use his updated version of the myth as our point of reference. The inbuilt desire of humanity to achieve its full potential seem to lead us into states of perpetual conflict with each other. In *Prometheus Unbound* the Holy Spirit is seen to work gently and with intelligence, effecting a shift from the need for external authority into a new state of being in which the authority is internal, man is 'sceptreless, free, uncircumscibed', and he becomes 'king over himself'. In the process, Prometheus renounces hatred and releases himself from bonds which are fundamentally self-imposed. However, Shelley emphasizes that the liberated man is still subject to restrictions and limitations, which he must now undertake to acknowledge without the commandments of a higher authority.

If we return to the definition of Daat as a point 'where the divine will can intervene directly in existence', we can see that there is more to be said about the role of the Holy Spirit. I have spoken about it as a threshold which we can cross if we have faith and are prepared to surrender; I have discussed the role of grace and hope in resolving conflict. There is something else, and that is miracle making. One of Chiron's most notable pupils was Asclepius who became the god of medicine; he not only healed the sick but he recalled the dead to life. This rare authority over death is also attributed to Jesus who is often depicted being visited by the Holy Spirit in the form of a dove. The Kabbalist's view seems to be that Divine Intelligence has created a basic pattern, using ten archetypes, on which all creation is founded; this pattern underlies everything and the interaction and variation between the ten are sufficient to create the extraordinary diversity of the entire universe. But the creative process has also set up a loop-hole, a space where variety and surprise can be introduced — if the ten archetypes were only ten then everything would be, eventually, predictable. This little extra allows a gap which releases us from a pre-determined creation. Daat is the equivalent of Heisenberg's 'Uncertainty Principle' — it is the room in which Schrodinger can put his cat and never know whether it will be dead or alive when he opens the door.

In the Yogic tradition, meditators who reach the state of transcendence perform 'sidi' techniques — during their state of deepest stillness they take up an idea and concentrate on it, with the intention to bring the idea into manifestation. This is the secret to achieving unusual feats such as levitation. When the mind is in the gap between the inner and the outer it is contact with the field of all possibilities, for which modern physicists have coined the word 'quantum field'. In this field the physical universe can be influenced by thought. No wonder Prometheus was crucified for encroaching into this space — it is mysterious and sacred, a 'sanctum sanctorum'.

In the Jewish tradition, the Ark of the Covenant was kept in an innermost apartment of the temple, the Holy of Holies, into which only the high priest was allowed to enter, and then only once a year on the Day of Atonement, Yom Kippur. Whenever their enemies desecrated this place they expected to find some treasure, but the Jews understood the secret power of the empty space and would not have placed anything in it of material worth. We have returned to the gap between heaven and earth represented in Michelangelo's painting. This space is pregnant with unknown possibility, with creative potential. When we ascend the Tree of Life and meet the Holy Spirit we surrender to this creativity and become co-creators with the Divine Intelligence. If we enter into this partnership with pure intention, then we participate in the process of miracle making. Then healing ourselves, and our planet, becomes a simple exercise, based on the surrender of personal will, in the face of compassion for the needs of the wider community of the human race, for the planet and the flora and fauna which share it with us.

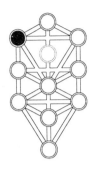

8

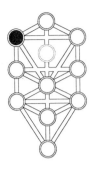

ZAPHKIEL

THE COMPASSIONATE

I am the rose of Sharon,
And the lily of the valleys.

Song of Solomon 2:1

As we rise into the uppermost branches of the Tree we come to meet the three Archangels which sit on the supernal Sephiroth, and are regarded as a creative triad by the Kabbalists. The triad is composed of Kether, the Crown, the White Head, which is on the central pillar and therefore neutral; Binah, Understanding, the essential feminine principle, the Mother; and Hochmah, Wisdom, the essential masculine principle, the Father. The Hebrew letter ‏ש‎ is used as a code for these three. The sound of this letter is 'sh', and we might well approach these three with hushed reverence.

The first of the three we can contact, using the traditional route, is Binah. The Archangel we find here is Zaphkiel, Angel of Contemplation. By this stage in my personal ascent I had begun to feel that I might be entering into a realm which was so abstract that my only visual impressions would be of colours, with no real form to speak of. I was surprised to find myself standing by a calm sea, stretching as far as I could see. The water was rippling with tiny waves trimmed with white foam. The sky above was a soft blue and the water a transparent bluegreen. I stood on sand with my feet on the very edge of the sea, which gently bathed them. The sound of the water swished and chuckled and there seemed to be a very faint breeze. I felt extraordinarily peaceful and my consciousness expanded into the calm air and water, as though I was totally united with the scene. I felt a great sense of delight and stretched my arms out and upwards. As I did so I saw what I took to be creatures rising from the sea to imitate me, but the creatures were flowers, pink rosebuds which opened into blossoms as they emerged. One of the roses stretched up and up and its petals expanded into the sky until I could hardly see any blue. I could hear faint voices singing, as in a Gregorian chant.

Then the centre of the rose became a woman's face with a blissful smile and a halo of pink light, and the petals became wings encircling the face, dainty wings with finely-etched feathers. The sky behind her twinkled with gold and silver stars which sent spinning rays of light into all the spaces which were not filled with her own rosy aura... I was quite entranced and had no desire at all to return to my everyday surroundings, nor any notion of the length of time I was held in that state of bliss with the Angel.

When John Blackwood*, the poet and metaphysician, came across my report of this vision he showed me one of his own poems, *Seamarks: Cambridge*, written in 1962-3. The following extract calls on the same imagery for the self-same archetype:

> *And the children recited in rhyme,*
> *The Sea is where*
> *The stoat and the hare,*
> *The peacock in pride,*
> *The dove in meekness,*
> *Go side by side,*
> *And what they say*
> *Is the fragrance of roses,*
> *Foundering upon a sea of roses,*
> *Motherhood made immaculate,*
> *Crystal roses, dividing and subdividing, ecstatic.*

When I first came across the title *Angel of Contemplation* I had a visual idea of a Buddha's face, serene, composed, asexual. I knew that this Archangel occupied a position on the 'feminine' pillar of the Tree but I was, all the same, surprised by the obvious femininity of the creature. Another reason for my surprise was that I had in the back of my mind that the planetary connection would probably be with Neptune, in Greek myth Poseidon, who is known as a tempestuous male monarch of the ocean. My lovely lady had certainly emerged from the sea, so I went in search of a Sea-Goddess.

Amphitrite was the reluctant wife of Poseidon. She was one of the many Nereids, the sea-nymphs who were daughters of Nereus, an old man of the Sea, a much older god than Poseidon. She was one of fifty sisters, among them Thetis, the mother of Achilles. Poseidon's first choice for a wife was Thetis but a prophecy that any son born to her would be greater than his father warned him off! He saw Amphitrite dancing on the island

---

* Please see the Afterword, page 112

of Naxos and sought her hand. Her response was to hide in the Atlas Mountains, until his messenger Delphinus won her over. For this success Delphinus was received into the starry constellations as the Dolphin.

Amphitrite plays a key role in the myth of Theseus who was provoked to plunge into the sea by Minos, the King of Crete, owner of the famous labyrinth with the Minotaur at its heart. Theseus' mother had been intimate with Poseidon as well as her own husband, Aegeus, although Poseidon had relinquished any claim to the child. King Minos threw a golden ring into the sea, challenging Theseus to prove that Poseidon had been his father by retrieving it. Amphitrite sent the Nereids to search for the ring and gave Theseus a jewelled crown, her wedding gift from Aphrodite. Theseus later married Ariadne, who had helped him solve the labyrinth with a golden ball of thread, and Ariadne wore the jewelled crown which had been brought up from the depths of the ocean.

The myths of the sea have something in common with the myths of the underworld: they involve deep searches which produce treasures, usually after the hero has fulfilled an impossible task. In most myths, and fairy stories, the tasks are beyond the capabilities of mortals and the protagonist is assisted by supernatural beings, old women, fairy creatures or, as in the story of Theseus, the inhabitants of another, deeper world. The sea nymphs find the ring and donate the wedding crown — from the water element; Ariadne helps Theseus conquer the Minotaur by providing the magic thread which guides him through the labyrinth — the earth element. Both the elements of earth and water are regarded as yin or feminine elements, and all of the helpers are feminine. Theseus then partakes in a wedding — an alchemical union in which the sea-crown is used as a reminder of the sovereignty of the unconscious. The story continues with Theseus' return home to his mortal father, King Aegeus of Athens. Theseus had promised to change the colour of his sails on his ship from black to white if he was safe. This small detail was forgotten in the joy of success and Aegeus, seeing the ships from a distance, with their morbid message - so he thought - threw himself, inconsolable, into the sea.

Theseus' error is often seen as a fateful flaw, a lack of care and consideration for other people, but it seems to me that Theseus had been transformed: he had slain the monster in the depths and had surrendered to the great spiritual ocean. Black and white are all the same to a person in a state of bliss. This 'mistake' is what we would call a Freudian slip — Theseus knows his time has come, he is a new man, he has been integrated with the feminine and is more suitable to reign than his father and after Aegeus' funeral Theseus unified the disruptive Athenians into a single state.

Amphitrite means 'to rub' or 'wear away on all sides'. This is what the sea does, it dissolves that which is solid, it can undermine structures and shift even rocks and mountains. Its processes can be gentle and persistent or dramatic and cathartic, but one way or another it is all pervasive. In astrology, nowadays we use Neptune (Poseidon) as a symbol of the dissolution of the personal self into the transpersonal. This dissolution may be effected by spiritual disciplines such as meditation or contemplation, or, negatively, by recourse to drugs or alcohol. This archetype, represented in the Kabbalist tree by Archangel Zaphkiel, is based on a desire for communion with the inward, yin, energy of the Holy Trinity, in which we return to our origins, deep in the quiet womb where consciousness is unmanifest, waiting to be born.

In Christian cosmology the Mother archetype is carried by the Virgin Mary. She is Theotokos, God-bearer, Mater Dei, mother of God, but also Stella Maris — star of the sea, the immaculate womb of the divine font, the primeval waters over which the Spirit moved. Her name carries the same etymology as 'mare', the sea. She has been worshipped for centuries by Catholics, often against the theological inclinations of the church hierarchy, and many great European cathedrals are named 'Notre Dame' after her. In 1950 the Pope proclaimed the *Munificentissimus Dei*, the dogma of the bodily ascent into heaven of the Virgin Mary — after nearly two millennia the Christians had eventually conceded the feminine contribution to the divine.

My vision of sea and roses was appropriate for an archetype carrying the Divine Mother or Mary impetus. The rose has long been associated with the Virgin, who has been called 'The Mystical Rose'; she was seen with roses by Bernadette of Lourdes, who was encouraged by the Virgin to use the 'rosary', a string of prayer beads named after a rose-garden. The oriental equivalent is, I suppose, the lotus, and both flowers have an exquisite quality about, delicate colours and an aura of serenity about them. The rose is softer, the petals have a rounded edge, whereas the lotus has a stiff quality, and seems more formal. The rose is also, probably, more famous for its perfume than the lotus.

After these ruminations on the rose I began to feel that it was a better contender for a symbol of contemplation than the lotus — especially as Zaphkiel seemed to be linked with Mary and thus with the mother's womb. I reminded myself that as I had been brought up, however unconsciously, in the Western tradition, then my images of the archetypes were likely to produce symbols from Western culture. Then an odd 'coincidence' brought be up sharp — so to speak. I had just finished writing the last paragraph when I made a short trip in my car and happened to put on the radio. The programme was 'Gardener's Question Time', the subject was roses! The question being discussed was how to deal with thorns — I had been so blissed out on my vision of the soft pink rose, with its velvety petals, that

I had forgotten the thorns! I returned to the Kabbalist's Tree – the left pillar, containing yin energy, is known as the Pillar of Severity, so perhaps the rose thorns add another dimension to this symbol. The womb of mother is a place of deep peace and serenity; it contains the unborn in a soft, watery environment where there is no sense of personal identity. But this transpersonal state cannot last, as William Blake reminds us; the state of innocence has to be replaced by experience which in turn leads to wisdom. The ovum has to be pierced by the sperm, the womb has to open to release the baby, the baby has to leave its mother's breast and eventually cut her apron strings — without these changes there is no creativity. The rose has a thorn, there is pain attached to beauty, there is severity even in compassion. Blake speaks of 'the invisible worm' which invades the rose:

> *O Rose, thou art sick!*
> *The invisible worm*
> *That flies in the night,*
> *In the howling storm,*
> *Has found out thy bed*
> *Of crimson joy:*
> *And his dark secret love*
> *Does thy life destroy.*

William Blake, The Rose

The erotic implications of the imagery are obvious: desire leads to conception, which in turn leads to death. But death means a return to the transpersonal; this is the natural cycle of creativity and the Archangel Zaphkiel is a reminder of containing power of the feminine which has to be broken for life to begin but to which we all return. In *I Ching* the second hexagram, The Receptive, would equate with this archetype; the attribute of this hexagram is devotion and it waits to be activated by the Creative (the first hexagram): 'It is the Creative that begets things, but they are brought to birth by the Receptive.' The image for The Receptive is earth and *I Ching* speaks of 'Nature's richness to nourish all living things'. We are back to Mother again — Mother Nature, Gaia, Pacha Mama, Notre Dame. In her mothering aspect she is the Black Madonna with her child; in her self-contained aspect she is the serene Virgin, dressed in pastels with roses at her feet, contemplating the Divine, awaiting the Beloved:

> *As the apple tree among the trees of the wood, so is my beloved among the sons. I sat down under his shadow with great delight, and his fruit was sweet to my taste.*
> *He brought me to the banqueting house, and his banner over me was love.*

Song of Solomon, Chapter 2:3-4

Zaphkiel's role is identical with the sufficient unto herself Virgin: we must be aware of the still potential contained here. Beyond the transcendental state of no thought which we entered at Daat, there is a deep, quiet space which holds myriad possibilities, but which cannot unfold its power independently of its opposite and complementary archetype, represented by the Archangel Raziel.

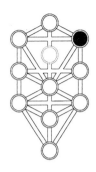

9

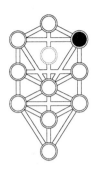

RAZIEL

THE WISE

Immortal, invisible, God only Wise,
In Light inaccessible, hid from our eyes.

Hymns Ancient & Modern

Now we are reaching further into the deepest metaphysics of creation: the Sephiroth Hochmah represents the potency of the Father principle, powerful but formless. This is the second attribute of the Creative Principle which is unfolding into manifestation, the male or active principle in the mysterious upper triad of the Tree. The Hebrew name for God in this particular disguise is Jehovah, meaning Essence of Being. Here we have an unmistakably patriarchal, Old Testament style character whose energy, when received suddenly and directly, can knock the recipient off balance in more ways than one. It contains pure Wisdom and is experienced by human beings as inspiration, sudden insight or revelation. This is the source of visions and intuitive knowledge, and the Archangel in charge is Raziel.

After some hunting I came across a small book which told the following story. According to the Hebrew tradition, when Adam and Eve were expelled from the Garden of Eden the Archangel Raziel gave Adam a book containing herbal knowledge, and setting out cures for all the illnesses which might beset humanity in its fallen state. This story is indicative of the activity of this archetype: it brings wisdom, or knowledge, which is not slowly or painstakingly accumulated by logical steps but is suddenly and completely realized. It is a visionary and awakening archetype. The work of Edward Bach who discovered the Flower Remedies is an example of this intuitive discovery. Creative artists and scientists will speak of sudden insights, the 'Eureka!' of Archimedes being the most famous case of all time. Anyone on the receiving end of this experience will describe it as a sudden illumination, as though a blind or shutter had been removed from a window and the sun had burst in. Raziel is also said to have revealed the mysteries of the Kabbala to Adam: he gave him insights into the metaphysical structure of life itself, thus equipping humanity to have direct involvement in the creative process. All prophetic insights and revelations have their source in this matrix, but the energy can be too hot to handle — like live electric current, it is exciting and enlivening, but potentially very dangerous. When we meet the angel Raziel we are coming close to the source of pure dynamic power at Kether, the Crown, which is at the top of the Tree, immediately above Hochmah. The Kabbalist describes the descent of divine energy as a lightning flash and at this point the descent has only just begun, the current has not been 'earthed', or taken on form — this will begin at Binah — and the energy is raw. Be aware! Shimon Halevi states that Hochmah provides the function of the Inner Intellect:

This is the deepest part of the mind, the highest intellectual centre from which emanates silent thought. From this potent area the most profound ideas and observation come. This centre sees with the inner eye of illumination, and speaks without words, as Wisdom.

There seems no doubt that Hochmah, via Raziel, provides us with our prophets and seers. It is a complementary energy to that of Binah — heavenly Father rather than heavenly Mother — which may explain why the Old Testament prophets have given us a patriarchal image of God, this being the source of their insights. I suspect that Raziel was the angel which appeared to Moses:

And the angel of the LORD appeared unto him in a flame of fire out of the midst of a bush: and he looked, and, behold, the bush burned with fire, and the bush was not consumed.

Exodus 3:2

This visitation heralded the voice of God and when Moses complained that he was not eloquent he was told:

I will be with thy mouth, and teach thee what thou shalt say.

Exodus 4:12

Nonetheless poor old Moses was overwhelmed by nerves and the Lord had to press-gang Aaron, Moses' brother, to act as the Divine mouthpiece while Moses made signs with a rod. It seems that contact with the intensity of Raziel makes a man dumb, as though direct revelation is beyond words. The Prophet Mahomet also complained, when told to 'Recite!', that he was unlettered and therefore incapable. The language of the Koran is regarded as the finest poetry in the Arab language, as though it had come from the very source of thought with no interference from the prophetic man.

I struggled for some days to put myself in the way of a vision of this Archangel. I met an Old Testament prophet, a Greek philosopher and a Renaissance magus with a pile of dusty books. None of these images had intensity of colour and light which I had come to recognize as the hallmark of a real archetype. I knew what my problem was — I was too nervous of the potential of this energy to be able to align myself with it. Our Western intellectual training insists that the discovery of new information or the invention of new projects are achieved by step-by-step logical procedures. We do admit that some people are geniuses and seem to have flashes of insight, but say that 'discovery favours the prepared mind' — we believe there is no short cut to wisdom. The archetype we meet at Hochmah, personified in the Archangel Raziel, presents information directly, or proposes what most people consider eccentric methods for discovery. Edward Bach's intuitive methods are a fine example, once he gained the insight he 'knew' the answers, without any logic or empirical evidence.

For the most part, people who offer knowledge gleaned directly from the Divine Source are ridiculed and seen as religious nutcases, and sometimes there is some justification for the scepticism they meet. Such information is only received by people who are able to open themselves to it and this involves setting aside the usual mental structures which tie us to more conventional thought patterns. Meditation and spiritual exercises are one way of doing this and, no doubt, the genius wrestling with a difficult formula or philosophical problem is exercising his mind in a similar way. But dramatic examples are found among people whose personality structures are disintegrating for one reason or another — the use of 'recreational' or medically prescribed drugs, or mental illness. Often such people make claims to have had religious insights, to be hearing the word of God and there is no doubt this is true; however the receiver is in such poor shape that the messages are scrambled along with all kinds of personal material which may be dredged up from their own unconscious. If there is any sense of personal coherence then the individual may be able to sift out the messages which are universal and qualify to be important insights. My own visions in 1974 may have been activated by the prescription of steroid drugs for an attack of asthma, their effect probably exaggerated by the fact that I had recently learned transcendental meditation and my physical system had become more sensitized. But the philosophical background I had, learning meditations, and many years of interest in comparative religion and mysticism gave me an advantage — I accepted the idea that some people have visions even if other people don't believe in them. I voyaged through spiritual realms normally inaccessible, but had to battle with the possibility of complete mental chaos. During my researches afterwards I came across the following lines in Maxime Rodinson's biography of the Prophet Mahomet:

'Those modern psychiatrists who hold religious beliefs are troubled, too, by these hallucinations and ecstatic states since, in all honesty, they are forced to admit that no clear distinction exists between the experiences of the mystics and those of the mentally ill. In the last analysis, the real distinction lies in the personalities of those who undergo the experience. On the one hand are weak personalities with impoverished and disconnected ideas, whose mental activity is petty and blundering. On the other are great minds with a forceful, well-integrated personality, capable of broad, far-reaching ideas and often intense, constructive mental activity, who use their mystical experiences as a basis for their own fresh and boldly individual philosophy.'

I would add that the mind-set of the receiver plays a large part in the way the experiences will unfold. A mind which is trained in Western materialistic philosophy, which says 'if I can't verify my experience by seeing or touching, or by comparing it with those around me, it therefore has no reality and no value', is bound to be both doubtful and fearful of any surreal thoughts or experiences. Fear creates negative thought patterns and then the very devil is let loose in a highly volatile situation; the measure between enlightenment and madness is a hair's breadth and the balance will be tipped by faith or fear. Many notable accounts of the mystical journey speak of the adventurer having to pass through hellish regions and wrestle with demons. The mystic requires great courage when treading where few have ventured before.

Eventually I met Raziel during a meditation. I saw a very fine cobweb like structure made of tiny filaments of light — like fibre optics, only even more delicate. These fibres seemed to hum and tinkle, vibrating at a very high speed. I felt that each one might be saying a different sound or word, if only I was on the same wavelength to hear them. The cobweb opened up in the centre and I saw the faint outline and form of a face which seemed at once very young and very old — and very knowing. It was a very serene face but it had an intensity about it, a slight sharpness which removed it from being totally peaceful, like a Buddha. The head was swathed in pale blue lights, folding and turning, and the fibres which had parted made a radiant halo which continued to vibrate and flicker. The eyes were a startling blue and as I looked into them I could see stars and shining galaxies stretching into an infinite distance. It was quite brilliant — and I was quite terrified!

In astrology this archetype is symbolized by Uranus, sky-god *par excel-*

lence, known as the awakener, the magician, and as the bringer of enlightenment. The planet Uranus was discovered in 1781, during a period of many upheavals and rebellions, the overthrow of monarchies, the struggles for the abolition of slavery and the rights of workers. The bringer of change was at first seen as a destroyer. In Greek myth the father figure Uranus is in a state of perpetual copulation with the mother figure, Gaia, and this union is brutally severed by Saturn, son to Uranus, who deprives his father of his male organ with his sickle. In this marriage of male and female, creative and passive, we see the fusion of superconscious and conscious but when Saturn — who represents Time — interferes the Uranian ability to fertilize comes to an end. This is the expulsion from the Garden of Eden — spirit and matter are, seemingly, separated. Again we meet the image of the worm or the thorn in the rose. However, Time is essential if creations are to come into actuality; before Saturn commits his heinous amputation Gaia's children have no opportunity to be born, they are kept in the womb. On the other hand, the separation means that we, as dwellers in a temporal world, can only make contact with the superconscious by shifting, however briefly, out of the time zones into the timeless. We should also note the epilogue to this myth. The dismembered phallus of Uranus falls into the sea and creates the foam from which the goddess Venus is born. Here we see an extension of the symbolism of the development of consciousness — the deep realms of the unconscious, represented by the sea, are fertilized by the divine seed from the superconscious and manifested into the archetype of love and healing. In Archangel tradition it is Raziel who has the knowledge to give the healer but it is Raphael who effects the cure at a practical level, and is actually on the scene directing Tobit with the healing process.

In astrological parlance Uranus is the 'higher octave' of Mercury. In other words it has a similar function in that it is an archetype which relates to thought and creativity, but the vibration is much faster. As one astrologer put it, 'Here the versatile is raised to the volatile. Uranus does not merely surprise he astonishes. Not content with showing us existing roads he cuts a channel through the mountains where nobody thought a road could be made.' (Charlotte Macleod: *Trusting, Astrology for Sceptics*.) We could say the same for the relationship between Gabriel and Raziel: Gabriel is a much safer Archangel to contact if you are looking for inspiration or hoping to start a creative project. If you open yourself to any of the supernal archetypes you may get landed with a task larger than you bargained for — they have a habit of totally disregarding the personal life that most of us have to get on with. Raziel's energy is also likely to bring magical surprises: all the remarkable happenings in the Old and New Testaments, such as the parting of the sea, the transformation of a rod into a serpent, the raising of the dead, are due to this vibration which, because it is not yet earthed, has a great transformative capacity. In Raziel the idea becomes the actuality in the twinkling of an eye — it acts directly on thought processes and has the ability to perform miracles by acting at a deep level in the psyche and in the material world. It is worth noting that the societies in the world which have been most involved in developing technology and equipment and the skills designed to solve problems as quickly as possible, or satisfy desires immediately, are those who cleave to a patriarchal image of the Divine. The Mother image is much more familiar among groups who are still close to the land and the gently unfolding processes of Nature. But these are both only attributes of the Divine and by the time we have reached the real powerhouse of the Tree of Life, the Crown from which the descent towards the Kingdom begins, we are back on the central pillar, where the energy is neither male nor female.

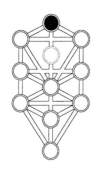

10

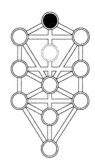

METATRON

THE POWERFUL

'The First Realm' is the Realm of 'Am I not your Lord?' This is the Realm
where you were before your physical existence, in the form of an atom
among a crowd of spirits... Then, when you descended from the pinnacle of
the world of spirits to the depths of the world of bodies, you forgot that
Realm and what happened to you in it. And if you turn to God search-
ingly, you will remember, God willing, your affirmation of his Lordship.
And you will say:

> *'I bore witness to you as King before our existence*
> *'Through what the eye saw in a handful of atoms,*
> *'A particular witness whose being I now understand.*
> *'At the time of testimony there was no deception,*
> *'The road I took was plainly and joyfully taken.*
> *'I was not a prisoner in the grip of confinement.'*

Shaykh Ibn'Arabi, Journey to the Lord of Power

The last step in our journey is at once the grandest and the least, since it
brings us both to the heights and back to the depths. We shift, finally, to
the quiet power at Kether, the Crown, from whence all the dynamic energy has emerged: it is the seed and the glory of all creation. The Archangel who sits here is named Metatron; like its counterpart at the root of the
Tree, Sandalphon, the name is Greek, rather than Hebrew.

In old texts Metatron is called 'The Angel of the Presence' but if we
translate from the Greek we get something infinitely more telling. 'Meta'
is used in various senses, chiefly 'sharing, action in common, pursuit or
quest and especially change (of place, order, condition, or nature) *Oxford
English Dictionary*. We find it as a prefix in 'metanoia', spiritual change,
and in 'metamorphosis', physical transformation. This archetype is in a
position of eminence, first in line to put creativity into action. It can be

seen as the source of Divine action; the place from which we emerge and the place to which we return; Alpha and Omega; the still centre of the turning world; the Grail. So the prefix 'meta' is entirely appropriate at many levels of meaning. This Archangel contains the dynamic to charge all the activity of the manifesting universe: it is raw, unformed creativity holding all possibilities in balance and therefore enables choices and transformation to take place. I thought, at first, that the suffix 'tron' simply implied 'throne', which would of course be suitable. However in my etymological searches I came across an archaic word 'tron': a public weighing machine found in cities and towns in the Middle Ages. Since Metatron is at the point of balance this would be an interesting verbal link: it may be that ' tron' and 'throne' are connected in meaning, since the person on the throne was always the final arbiter in disputes and would weigh the evidence in legal cases. This interpretation dovetails nicely with suggestions from old texts that the name was derived from the Latin 'metator', a guide or measurer. The suffix 'tron' is found in the word 'electron' — if 'meta' is 'change', we could translate Metatron as 'particle changer'. In any case Metatron sits on a mighty throne and is able to transform those who come before it.

My own journey up the Tree of Life had been provoked by the visionary experiences I had in 1974, the culmination of which was an occasion when I was overwhelmed by a light of such awesome power that I was convinced that it was an Archangel. The light seemed to either enter at, or emanate from, my head, before filling the whole body and eventually intensifying near the base of the spine and then rushing upwards, back into the head. This description has led several people to suggest to me that the light indicated the opening of the Crown chakra and the upward movement was Kundalini rising. Anyone who knows the yogic model of the chakras will see the similarities it bears to the Tree of Life. Certainly if the human body is seen in terms of the Tree then there is a direct channel up the central column, from the base or root of the Tree, which opens up at the top — called the Crown in both models. I could describe my experience either as an opening of the Crown chakra, or as a meeting with Metatron — either way it was a knockout!

In the weeks that followed my experiences I was also in touch with other archetypal energies, which is why I find the Tree of Life with the communicating world of the Archangels so helpful as a model. It seems, in retrospect, that the initial opening drew me up into the supernal triad where I spent time feeling totally blissful and contemplative — with Zaphkiel — and time receiving concepts, ideas and knowledge about things past and future — with Raziel — as well as moments when I was able to perform, consciously and unconsciously, various minor miracles —

Metatron. The lower branches of the tree had been left behind in the process and I had no sense of rootedness, which is why my state of spirituality was of such concern to my family. Both the Kabbalist and the Yogi would say that sudden contact with higher realms would be likely to create dramatic and unsettling manifestations in the psyche — generally translated as mental illness by the medical profession. Anyone who finds themselves in unknown territory needs a map and a guide, and since the medics do not allow any reality to the inner world they are hardly likely to be able to provide suitable tools or guidance. I was fortunate that I met a Sufi at that time who gave me some very handy tips for my travels.

Metatron is the Archangel at Kether, the first Sefiroth which emanates from the Ayin Sof Or, the Endless Light which surrounds the Void. The Supreme Deity is an incomprehensible principle which is only to be discovered by eliminating all its cognizable attributes, and we have arrived at this point, right at the very edge of the manifest universe. All the attributes are below us and here is Nothing and Everything. This is the place where Divine Intelligence says, 'Eheieh Asher Eheieh' — 'I am that I am'. It is the first point, a dot which contains all creation within it, it is pure divinity, uncontaminated, sexless, inscrutable. This principle cannot be personified but the Archangel acts as our bridge. Without it we cannot even hear the words 'I am that I am'; this is why we need Archangels, in order to have concepts about the Divine Attributes.

Traditional literature describes the 'great Metatron' as ancient, bearded and inspired but at the same time youthful, an eternal, radiantly beautiful adolescent. Isaiah's vision seems to have been of such a being:

> *I saw also the Lord sitting upon a throne, high and lifted up, and his train filled the temple.*

> *Above it stood the seraphims, each one had six wings; with twain he covered his face and with twain he covered his feet and with twain he did fly.*

> 6 1:2

We will have to forgive the visionaries of the past their continual use of the masculine pronoun for all angels. I believe it was something to do with their lack of education! Any creature which projects the intensity of light and energy that angels and Archangels have may be understood to be radiating masculine energy in a society in which feminine energy was allowed little real expression. This particular Archangel has strong masculine connections since tradition says that it was once the Prophet Enoch who was 'taken up' by God, crowned with God's own coronet and given seventy-two wings and innumerable eyes. His flesh was transformed into flame, his sinews into fire, his bones into embers, and he is surrounded by storm, whirlwind, thunder and lightning. Metatron sits on the throne with a Crown, but it tops the central pillar and is definitely neutral. Metatron may be described as the Lord of the Tree, but this Lordship does not require male energy; on the contrary it requires a perfect balance between masculine and feminine vibrations. In some sources the Shekinah is regarded as the female aspect of Metatron and called 'Matrona'. The Shekinah — from the Hebrew 'shachan', to reside — is the divine indwelling, the female manifestation of God, the 'bride of the Lord', comparable with the shakti of Shiva. She is the Liberating Angel, the glory or 'effulgence' of God. At the top of the Tree of Life she is the Queen, and one Jewish haggadah says that she hovers over conjugal unions and blesses them with her presence. We see here that the ancient Jewish tradition continually refers back to the feminine even when we seem to be presented with the most patriarchal of archetypes. Metatron has a bride in constant union, until this aspect of God divides itself into two separate archetypes, Holy Mother (Zaphkiel) and Holy Father (Raziel).

While I was still in the process of writing the last chapter I had the following dream: I was in a beautiful garden, with wonderful flowers and plants, like an Arabian Paradise. Through the garden ran a glittering stream and on my side of the stream hovered all the Archangels I had written about. In the garden beyond the stream I could see Metatron as a brilliant white light topped with a golden crown, gleaming and sparkling with coloured jewels. I stood on my side willing the Archangel to come over, but it stayed put. I wanted to go across but the stream seemed to create an impasse. I woke from the dream without resolving the problem and wondered whether I would come up against the same difficulty when I asked to meet Metatron in a more conscious state. On the contrary, I think the dream had either set up a deep receptivity to the archetype or, more likely, was indicating that the next stage was about to unfold.

I had developed a system whereby I created an inner picture of the Tree, travelled from the very foot along the corridors and called on each Archangel in ascending order before asking to meet the next one in line. I put myself in a meditative state before doing this and usually found that the process seemed to happen through my whole body and not just in my head: in other words when I called up Sandalphon the energy seemed to move in my feet, while I was receiving a visual impression in my mind. The vision came into the mind whether the eyes were closed or not. In the case of Metatron the energy was centred around the top of my head — the crown. I saw a brilliant white-gold globe of light. I couldn't see any facial features but I felt that I was being watched. The globe radiated beams which seemed to stretch into infinity and there were rays of reds and golds which pushed upwards like a fountain from the top of the globe, spreading into a huge semi-circle of flames or feathers. There was a tremendous rushing noise and a beating sound, like a bass drum, which became louder and louder. As the drumming increased, the brilliant feathers created a vast shower of tiny coloured lights — rather like a particularly extravagant firework display — and each one seemed to be humming a different note, but all were in harmony. The drumming became louder and louder until it suddenly stopped. The silence was deafening by contrast; everything became very still and gradually the colours diminished until there was nothing left but brilliant white light:

I am frozen and time stands still
In the empty citadel,
No sound... no breath,
Until the first bell
Fragments eternity,
The first prism
Splinters the light,
The egg hatched,
The bird bright,
The first song
In Adam's Eden
And I AM there.

Reaching the top of the tree brings us to this point of perfection; all is annihilated yet all is waiting, ready for re-creation. This is the habitation of the phoenix, reduced to ashes so that it can rise again; it is a place of complete surrender and total transformation. In astrology this archetype is represented by Pluto. The story of the Prophet Enoch being scorched out of existence and being lifted up to a new identity as the Archangel is also quite in keeping with the dramatic and awe-inspiring activities which astrologers associate with Plutonian activities. Astronomically it is the most distant planet; it is thought to be solid throughout and in a state of permanent freeze. Mythologically, Pluto is the God of the Underworld and holds sway over the dead, the powers of darkness and all things under the earth. As a judge he was severe and pitiless but scrupulously fair and could not be bribed by gifts, sacrifices or flattery. He was moved by the sound of Orpheus' lyre and would have restored the dead Eurydice to Orpheus had Orpheus not broken his rule and turned to see her before they left the Underworld. In another myth, Pluto stole the beautiful Persephone from the upper world and only agreed to give her back for part of the year after her mother, the Goddess Demeter, refused to make the Spring come again until her daughter was returned. Pluto strikes a very hard bargain — it's a question of 'you are either for me or against me'. He deals in absolutes because his power is absolute.

The God of Hades seems a very dark character besides the brilliance of Metatron but they do stand up to direct comparison. The old pictures of the Tree of Life which show the top branches under the earth tell us that Metatron lives in the same quiet depths as Pluto. The Crown of the Tree is the root of the next Tree; the dark earth contains the potential and the nutrition for new growth. Dead leaves rot into the soil and are transformed into the compost which feeds the growth of new leaves. In the dark god's dominion we find our wealth: all manner of precious minerals and jewels as well as the more pedestrian metals — tin, copper, iron — which we use to create the good things we enjoy having around us. A wealthy man is a 'plutocrat' and such men have power in our society; often they are dark gods, working secretly and sometimes with questionable methods. The great danger that astrologers see in the Pluto archetype is that its enormous power can be used for personal ends, to manipulate and take power over others; it is the source of Deep Magic just as the split atom produces immense power, and handling it demands scrupulous attention to moral and ethical duty. Perhaps it is the human inability to handle this power without selfishness which has seeded the myth of Pluto as a dark God — our mythology, after all, mirrors our own state of consciousness. The Greek version of this God, Hades, has a helmet of darkness with which to conceal his own brightness which would be too much for human eyes to bear. Maybe when we are prepared to surrender to the uncompromising, ego-less, demands of this archetype we will be able to look into the brightness of Metatron without fear and thus be renewed.

Creator

I am and I alone;
And in my Aloneness I choose to be Fire:
Stars blazing for my delight;
Fireflies glittering in the night.

I am Alone, I am.
And in my Aloneness I choose to be Earth:
Crystalline unfolding in my heart of rock and mountain,
Stirring the landscape into hill and valley from my volcanic
fountain.
I only am, I alone
And in my Aloneness I choose to be Air.
The rush inward and outward of wind, of lung's breath.
Spirit... Paraclete... Now Life... Now Death.

I am the Alone, I,
And in my Aloneness I choose to be Water:
The Ocean, drop by drop.
The baptismal rain. The river and every stream.
In Jordan's river, I again.

Surrender! Where I am there is no other:

I scorch, I bury, I blast, I drown,

I live.

I felt an enormous sense of completion when I had reached the goal of my travels, like arriving at the top of a mountain, or finishing a garment — an experience with which I am more familiar! However the mountaineer always has to make a descent. The Persian poet 'Azizi criticizes the seeker who is only interested in the ascension, whose aim is the transcendent alone. Perfection requires immanence also:

It is no more than two steps
to the Friend's door —
You have stopped
at the first step.
So the story is not quite complete, the last stage is yet to come.

THE DESCENT

...and whatsoever you see of spiritual forms and of things visible whose countenance is goodly to behold and whatsoever you see of thought, imagination, intelligence, soul and the heart with its Secret, and whatsoever you see of Angelic aspect, or things whereof Satan is the spirit... Lo! I, the 'Perfect Man', am that whole, and that whole is my theatre... The sensible world is mine, and the Angel world is of my weaving and my fashioning.

Abdul Karim Jili, The Perfect Man

The process in which the mystic, or shaman, engages, requires an inner journey. We started our travels at the foot of the Tree of Life and made our progress upward. When we arrived at our destination we merged, temporarily, with the Oneness of the Creator. We cannot stay in this state of bliss – we have to make our Descent. Teresa of Avila speaks of an interior castle in which she enters room after room until she eventually arrives at the central room, bright as a diamond, the turning point of the inner world. Christians often use the Stations of the Cross as a symbolic map of the spiritual journey. Mahomet described his own night journey, during which he visited Jerusalem, the Holy City and the seven Heavens. But whatever religious symbolism or terminology is involved, the key issue is that transcendence alone is not enough: the traveller has to come back to earth and live in the world. It is the grounding part of the experience which validates it : this is the main criterion for determining whether the recipient of the visions is a genuine mystic or a psychotic. The reality of the experience can be measured in its effectiveness - by the actual difference it makes in the day-to-day world. The Persian poet Azizi warns that transcendence is not enough:

> *It is no more than two steps to the Friend's door – you have stopped at the first step.*

Teresa told her nuns to remember that God is also in the pots and pans – not just in the private space provided by the cell, or in the mysticism of the Mass, but in the everyday tasks, shared by the community.

Beyond Metatron is Endless Light which we cannot enter until we have surrendered our physical bodies. There is little point in hovering on the edge, hoping for the inaccessible, so we might as well make our descent, taking with us as much of the radiance that we have collected on the way as possible Perhaps we can share it around, like Jack when he came down from the Beanstalk.

The Kabbalists' descent of the divine is the lightning flash, and we can well imagine it as a rapid but flowing process, moving from one collection point to another, hopefully without any blockages on the way. The powerhouse has been established at the top at Metatron. This Archangel holds the energy which will provide the dynamic for the rest of the system. All is in balance. The energy is contained in a very dense form and in order for it to be released there has to be a schism, just as the fertilized ovum divides in order for creativity to unfold into a human being. We could call Metatron the Archangel of the Atom — it contains the immense power which underlies all the activity in the universe. There is light, but no form.

With the first division comes light and dark, masculine and feminine, and the supernal triad is established. The Sky God and the Queen of the Heavens, Jehovah and Mary, Raziel and Zaphkiel. The three Great Archangels between them have the power to make things happen. Metatron provides the energy, Raziel the seed, and Zaphkiel the nourishment. Perhaps we should re-word the Lord's Prayer and address it to the three of them, thereby acknowledging that our spiritual parenting comes from an archetypal foundation which extends beyond the Father archetype.

Next we pass through the veil which separates the transpersonal from the personal. A child contained in the womb is still a cosmic being, the mother carries it but cannot yet lay claim to its person, it dwells in a silent world of it own. It is becoming manifest but is not yet born. Here is the quiet space where the Holy Spirit works silently, giving spirit to that which is, as yet, only a concept being nourished; the mystery is held in secrecy in the Holy of Holies, before activity begins. But we have to venture onward; we have to be born, we have to leave Paradise and move into the world.

Zadkiel supports and comforts us in our infancy, while we are still innocent and prepared to rest in its wings. This is the traditional role of Father as provider; its task is also to encourage and protect us. People who meet this protective archetype sometimes feel that they don't have to do anything for themselves: 'God will provide therefore I can just sit back'. The Father archetype provides a firm foundation but we have to take responsibility for ourselves. We need to gain experience along our journey; duty, discipline and self-control must be taken on board if we are to accept joyously the severity of Samael.

Samael's task is to demonstrate the laws of karma, to show us how to live in the world of time: it makes schedules and house rules and takes measures to ensure they are implemented. If we learn these rules we understand how to live correctly and in harmony with the universe: we regulate our own behaviour and set up our own limitations. Samael is not a harsh parent nor does it create evil, only we always tend to push the limits to see how far we can go and then we get our knuckles rapped. Like a good teacher it will only give positive criticism and its reprimands will be appropriate. However, we need to listen — this Archangel is the most exacting and demanding from the point of view of personal development; if we don't heed the lessons being offered, the tap on the shoulder may turn into a hammering. Because of the nature of karmic law the punishments are sometimes taken on board by other generations: 'The sins of the father are visited on the sons,' and we are unable to see the obvious cause and effect. Then we speak of bad luck and ask how can there be a God who is good when such terrible things happen to innocents? According to tradition, Samael has been given control over planet earth while the human race is growing up. You had better get on good terms with this stern parent, honour the rules that have been set, and recognize that commandments and prohibitions have sound natural precepts behind them. Otherwise you will continue to find that all your personal plans will be subject to interference from unexpected sources; the human race is evolving rapidly and the karmic repercussions of behaviour will raise their heads with equal rapidity.

The next leg of our journey brings us back to the central pillar: in fact to the key position of the lower part of the Tree. Here we have a hot line to the divine energy, via the central channel which soars upwards —Michael is in direct line of descent from Metatron. This is the seat of our own Higher Self, the Christ within, sitting in glory. It is Michael's task to harness the disparate vibrations of the seven Archangels 'who stand before the throne'. It acts as the charioteer, taking the reins of the horses so that they act together rather than pulling in different directions. Michael represents the individualizing power within the psyche and we need Michael's energy to help us focus our own centre, to take up our own sovereignty. Here is our anchor, the stability and certainty we require before moving further downwards.

Next we meet Hanael. It will provide ongoing motivation and persistence so that the creative vision will be maintained. It adds drive and urgency so that the task in hand will not be overlooked. Hanael is a protector and only becomes a warrior when creativity is threatened. Then the display of persistence may appear to be aggressive, depending on your point of view. It will defend us, like a big brother, and like a sibling its activity is based on tribal loyalty; it is not there to criticize but to support. Its opposite number is Raphael and the two of them can be seen in terms of 'will' and 'love', polarities which are very difficult to balance. This is where Michael's unifying work is so vital to our basic health, otherwise we become divided, continually pulled between 'I' and 'you'.

The feminine vibration of Raphael, gently hovering over our anxieties and pains, overflowing with solace, eases us when there is difficulty. It is a gentle sister, a friend in need. It makes things beautiful and opens our eyes to beauty, shifting our consciousness when we are tired so that we get glimpses of the exquisite harmony of the divine order.

Now we come back to the central pillar once more. Gabriel gives us our real humanity: it allows us to create and to communicate, and by these gifts we can know each other and our own self. This Archangel offers a mirror so that we may reflect on our divinity. When it comes to herald new ideas and fresh beginnings, it creates opportunities for insight and evolution. Only when we know ourselves truly can we come into our own, full potential and take up our role in the Kingdom.

The last step on the journey is to meet Sandalphon, Guardian of the Earth and its Bride, the Moon (see Appendix One: 'Auriel'). Sandalphon's task is fortified by all the other Archangels and underpinned by the immense energy of Metatron, for in one sense they are the same angel. In Kabbalist literature Sandalphon is also known as the Messias. This title implies a perfect balance, the divine and the human in harmony, but also the intimate and loving rulership of a power which has made a descent into the realm of Nature. The creativity we received from Gabriel is made manifest through Sandalphon: this is the place where we present that which we have made out of our thoughts. The child which has been born is presented at the Temple; it has to take up its stewardship. The manifest world, which we meet everyday when we open our eyes, represents our relationship with the Archangels and the collected being of the human race. It is a result of our activity; but our activity is a result of our thoughts, of our inner world, of our connection with, or disassociation from, the divine source of all creation. Is this world which we see good? I believe at present most of us would answer 'no'. But, at least, we have started to ask the question and search for the reasons why our world is not as beautiful, why our relationships are not as harmonious, why our work is not as satisfying, as our inner knowledge tells us it could be. The Archangels are making their presence felt. Look out for them, make friends with them, they only need a little encouragement and the whole world would be changed.

Tao

I walk the wild ways,
I fill the seasons.
I bud in the sticky spring,
I dust the yellow catkin.

I blaze in the rude red dahlia,
I blush in the soft-skinned rose.
I conquer, mahogany shining,
I twist and rustle in autumn woods,
Leave skeletons, Death.
Silence.

I glitter the diamond icicle.
Precise.
I drop the snow skirt.
Gentle.
I mother the quiet earth
Back to the birth.

APPENDIX ONE

AURIEL – THE BRIDE

And the Spirit and the Bride say, Come. And let him that heareth say, Come. And let him that is athirst come. And whosoever will, let him take the water of life freely.

Revelations 22:17

There are many Archangels whose functions are not included in the Kabbalist's system and the most notable of these is Auriel — sometimes spelled Uriel or Oriel. (Some sources identify Auriel/Oriel as a separate Archangel from Uriel but my work has led me to the conviction that they are one and the same. The prefixes Aur, Or and Ur all have the same meaning — golden; even urine is so called. because of its golden colour.) This Archangel is one of the four Archangels of the directions who are connected to the four elements: Michael's element is Fire, Raphael's Air, Gabriel's Water and Auriel's is Earth. Its name is variously translated as 'light' or 'fire' of God. Auriel is connected with the month of September and it was this discovery, coupled with its rulership of the Earth element that led me into some revealing visions and insights; I began to see that Auriel might represent the Bride of Sandalphon. Tradition gives a feminine aspect to Metatron, the Archangel of the Crown of the Tree and the Kabbala makes it clear that the Crown and the Kingdom are one — thus Sandalphon is the incarnation of Metatron at ground level. The feminine aspect of Metatron is the Shekinah and I believe we can incorporate Auriel into the scheme by aligning it with Sandalphon and giving it the Moon as its heavenly body. This would be in keeping with esoteric astrology which associates the Moon with the sign of Virgo, since Auriel is connected with the month of September; this feels even more appropriate when we note that Lady's Day, the Feast of the Virgin Mary, is held in September (usually on September 8th, when the Sun is halfway through the sign of Virgo). This suggestion does not resonate particularly well with some of the traditional stories of this Archangel, one of which says that it was once the prophet Uriah. However, many Uriel tales have also been assigned to other Archangels, notably Gabriel. Several accounts refer to Auriel disclosing mysteries either of 'the heavenly arcana' or of alchemy which would be in keeping with the feminine archetype of the Moon, and the poet Dryden describes Auriel ascending from heaven in a chariot drawn by white horses.

In astrology the Moon is associated with the unconscious and with the emotions over which we have little or no conscious control; if we look towards self-knowledge we are directed towards incorporating the unconscious and the conscious into a *whole* consciousness, from which we can act in perfect accord with the way things ARE. This state, the state of Bliss which is the basis of Right Action, can be symbolized by an inner marriage in which the conscious self takes the unconscious in perfect union; the King, or Messias, is wedded to the True Bride and the Kingdom is governed correctly. Then we arrive at 'a new heaven and a new earth' in which consciousness and matter no longer strive against each other but function harmoniously. The feminine is accepted and revered, she receives her Crown and her blessings are freely given. My vision of Auriel was not of a virginal bride in white gown and veil but of golden woman in regal dress wearing a crown of leaves and flowers. She was a creature of gifts, of fruitfulness, carrying a cornucopia overflowing with fruits of the earth. I thought she must be the equivalent of Ceres, the corn goddess, identified with Demeter, although both these goddesses are considered to be earth mothers. Perhaps she has more kinship with Hecate who was regarded by the Greeks as a goddess of the moon and was cousin to Artemis. Hecate was considered to have authority over the fertility of the earth and to bring wealth, success and good luck.

Although I feel strongly that the Archangels should be referred to with the neutral gender, it is very tempting, in this case to refer to Auriel as 'she'. In traditional writings the Shekinah is always referred to in the feminine and all Archangels have masculine pronouns, however this should not inhibit us from assigning attributes usually regarded as feminine to these archetypes. Nor should we be overwhelmed by the weighty concept of 'tradition', these archetypes belong to us all and we reveal more of their power and use by drawing on our own inner library, rather than by slavish reference to ancient manuscripts. In my personal journey I find Auriel to be both mother and Bride and find giving HER a part to play, as consort to Sandalphon, the Messias, both illuminating and satisfying.

APPENDIX TWO

ARCHANGELS AND

ASTROLOGICAL ARCHETYPES

1 Archangels and Planets

I have written at some length about the connections between the archetypes as represented on the one hand by the Archangels of the Tree of Life model, and on the other by the gods and goddesses of the Greek myths who we encounter in the astrological tradition. There are some issues which these comparisons raise which I want to deal with, as well as offering some ideas concerning the archetypes and the present state of humankind.

The Kabbalist tradition makes connections between the Sephiroth and the planets which do not fit with my suggestions. I have to say that I am not a Kabbalist, but I am a reasonably experienced astrologer and my observations about the Archangels and their traditionally accepted roles lead me to different conclusions, which I think can be justified. Of course it is only since the discoveries of Uranus, Neptune and Pluto that the Kabbalist has needed to consider the relationship of the top triad to planets at all, but the seven lower Sephiroth have been long associated with planetary vibrations and some of these do not make any sense when they are held up for close inspection with astrological tradition. It seems likely that the allocation of planets to Sefiroth dates back to Pico della Mirandola, a remarkable Renaissance philosopher. Pico was seen to be brilliant from an early age and became enthusiastic about the knowledge which was being made available to the Italian *cognoscenti* after the translations of old documents, such as the *Books of Hermes Trimagistus*. Pico called himself a Christian Kabbalist and tried to demonstrate the possibility of a synthesis between ancient wisdom and the Christianity of his day. However, Pico was not in favour of astrology; I suspect he saw it is as a flawed science which provided a pre-determined world-view – Pico's philosophy encouraged self-determination. It seems likely that his active dislike of astrology would have led to him disregarding the archetypes represented by the astrological gods, when he was trying to assign planets to the Sefiroth, and simply using their astronomical positions as a guide. In order to compare the Kabbalist's suggestions with my own here are two diagrams (see figures 6a and 6b, overleaf).

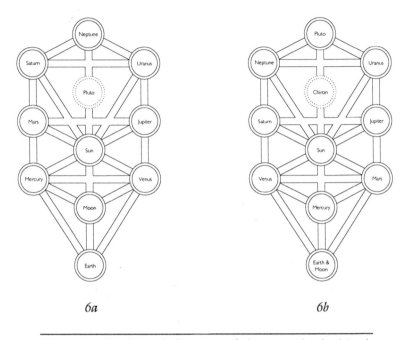

6a   6b

Figure 6a   Traditional allocation of planets to the Sephiroth

Figure 6b   Author's allocation of planets to the Sephiroth

The one particular difficulty that both astrologers and Kabbalists may find with my version of the model is that it suggests that Sandalphon relates to both the Earth and the Moon. I personally feel quite comfortable with this concept. The Moon is the Earth's satellite and belongs with the Earth. They have an intimate relationship, like husband and wife they are 'one flesh'. Astrologers offer the Moon as a symbol of the unconscious but the unconscious is not separate from our whole being, even if it is mysterious and elusive. Perhaps it is time we acknowledged the psychological unity of the outer, observable reality represented by the Earth itself and the inner realm of emotion and desire which underpins that reality, symbolized by the Moon. The stewardship of the planet — represented by Sandalphon — implies an understanding of the ebb and flow of the seasons, a harmonious connection with the living, growing processes which are nurtured by the Earth and the Moon acting together, as all dedicated gardeners will know. In the previous Appendix I have explained how the Archangel Auriel can be brought into the scheme and represents the Moon, as Sandalphon's bride.

Most of the other differences have been discussed in the appropriate chapters. Gabriel has obvious connections with Mercury. While I was writing this I came across an article on crop circles in which the author suggested that Gabriel could be identified with Hermes, and that the crop circles were a manifestation of Gabriel's heraldic energy. I quite agree with this suggestion, but the actual manifestation in the cornfields would require Sandalphon's assistance and the whole exercise would have been initiated at the top of the Tree. All ten Archangels are involved in the process of revelation.

It seems particularly strange that the Kabbalist associated Venus with a point on the active pillar of the Tree and Mars a point on the passive pillar. I think I can justify turning this around. Jupiter and Saturn do seem to be sitting on the right pillars but my version puts them directly opposite each other, which seems appropriate from the astrological point of view. I think the supernal triad has to equate to the three outer planets: Neptune is quite suitable for 'The Angel of Contemplation' at Binah; the activity of Uranus equates with that of Raziel at Hochmah and Pluto definitely fits neatly with the role of Metatron.

2   The Tree of Life and Mount Olympus

I have worked through a detailed comparison between the mythological gods and goddesses and the Archangels, chapter by chapter, but it is also worth looking at the two systems as whole concepts — i.e. how the archetypes relate to each other within the framework of the respective models. The Tree of Life presents a very exact structure in diagrammatical form, with a particular direction and a sense of unfolding from a seed to full flowering. The energy behind this growth is understood to emanate from a Divine Power which transcends the model, yet lends its power so that manifestation can take place — the Power is also immanent. The Divinity has set up the archetypes to function in a particular way — and that includes the one Archangel who tries to have it its own way, Samael, because in spite of its rebellion it is still retained as a functioning element. So the Tree of Life offers a model of balance and harmony, of correct interchange between the Archetypes who represent the various energies in the underlying structure of all consciousness and all manifestation. In the model offered by the court of Mount Olympus, there is no external Divinity breathing life into gods and goddesses. In the beginning, Mother Earth — Gaia — emerged out of Chaos, gave birth to her son Uranus as she slept and then gave birth to his children, the Titans. We are not told who fathered Uranus; the family starts with him and he remains within it. The dynastic struggles between the Olympians are well known and represent, in modern psychological astrology, the tensions between the archetypes who, in this model, are vying for supremacy. This is in stark contrast to the Kabbalist's model which has a hierarchy, but also a correct role for each archetype in relationship to its peers. We might see the Olympian scenario as a model of the way the archetypes actually do compete within the human psyche, each struggling to take sovereignty, and the Angelic hosts as a model of how they can relate correctly to each other, how they should be part of a harmonious whole and not pulling in different directions. What we need to understand very clearly is that until we put our inner kingdom in order the outer kingdom will suffer and our whole livelihood on the planet will be jeopardized. The precarious situation humanity is in will not be cured by legislation for recycling can and paper, or against CFCs, but by our own reconnecting with the Archangels who will shift us into a new mode of being. The physical harmony of the Earth depends on the attitude of those who dwell on it:

> *The spring, the summer,*
> *The childing autumn, angry winter change*
> *Their wonted liveries, and the mazed world*
> *By their increase now knows not which is which.*
> *And this same progeny of evils comes*
> *From our debate, from our dissension;*
> *We are their parents and original.*

A Midsummer Night's Dream II.i 111 - 117)

3 Archangels and present transits

The most notable configuration in the heavens at present is the conjunction between Uranus and Neptune in the sign of Capricorn; they first came into orb of conjunction in 1989 and will remain so until 1998; there was a period of particular intensity in 1993. Generally speaking, astrologers interpret this as a very trying combination: Neptune the Dissolver plus Uranus the Awakener in the sign of structure and government is bound to mean that old forms will be pulled apart and our psychological stability will be shaken, alongside the collapse of any systems which are too rigid to have any use in the coming 'New Age'. If we look at this conjunction as a collaboration between two great Archetypes represented by Zaphkiel and Raziel we may be able to find a slightly different perspective, which will add a new dimension to the astrological view. In the creative triad these two represent the Great Goddess, Queen of the Heavens, and the Sky God, Mother and Father to the archetypes on the lower branches. They are now in a state of union — communion — and are, hopefully, generating something fruitful which will be born when they leave the marriage bed. But the transformative power in the triad which fires the union is supplied by Metatron and we therefore need to keep a close eye on the activities of Pluto, in order to give us the whole picture. Pluto is presently moving through the last decanate of Scorpio — it will move into Sagittarius in January 1995 — and so we find the god of transformation in its own sign, long associated with sexuality and death, the ultimate transformation. Astrologers will make obvious connections between this placement and the plague of Aids: in this illness sex and death are inextricable, no longer 'petit mort' but 'grand mort'. Not only are Uranus and Neptune conniving to dissolve and shatter the structures of governments and bureaucracy, but Pluto creeps into the bed of dark desire, threatening our very existence if we break tryst with the most fundamental secret of being. This secret contains a deep magic: the body is a physical manifestation of the soul and every abuse of the body is an abuse of the soul who will, in turn, manifest an external reality which mirrors, exactly, that abuse. Human beings rape and pillage the planet and she begins to die before our eyes; human beings play decadent games with their own bodies and they see themselves fade away into ghastly creatures, the soul dies before the body, their houses are empty and there are no lights on. The archetypal energies are not concerned with 'morals', their purpose is creative and the issues are of balance and harmony. Many human beings abuse their bodies to a lesser or greater degree — we over-indulge ourselves with food, drink, sex. It is not that we have to become puritanical but that we have to pay due respect to the physical, to understand the body as a home for the soul and be good housekeepers, giving it loving attention and care. We don't have to give up physical pleasures — on the contrary, when we are balanced and whole we will have more pleasure from being physical creatures. All illnesses have a metaphysical base and we need to recognize our culpability and personal responsibility for the state of our own bodies and that of Mother Earth.

The Archangel Metatron is the balancer, sitting on the throne of judgement, and the sign of Scorpio allows this archetype to transform us even as it lays waste:

> *For even as love crowns you so shall he crucify you.*
> *Even as he is for your growth so is he for your pruning.*
> *Even as he ascends to your height and caresses your tenderest branches that quiver in the sun,*
> *So shall he descend to your roots and shake them in their clinging to the earth.*
> *Like sheaves of corn he gathers you unto himself.*

> *He threshes you to make you naked.*
> *He grinds you to whiteness.*
> *He kneads you until you are pliant;*
> *And then he assigns you to his sacred fire, that you may become*
> *sacred bread for God's sacred feast.*

Kahlil Gibran, *The Prophet*

The Angelic model allows us to see the three transpersonal planets as a powerful triad, who are presently combining forces to shake the deepest roots of our collective consciousness. Metatron is challenging our most intimate relationships, calling us to honour the sexual act as sacred and to recognize the potential every personal union has for individual and collective transformation. Zaphkiel and Raziel are offering a model of the creative marriage in which male and female energies work in harmony. The main reason that this conjunction heralds the kind of chaos we are seeing in Eastern Europe, is that most governmental structures are patriarchal and have been based for centuries on the dominance of leftbrained, analytical thinking. Now it is essential that we find a way to balance yang and yin energies and develop new approaches to running our economic and social lives, so that all people will feel that a Compassionate Mother is at home as well as a Wise Father.

APPENDIX THREE

ARCHANGELS AND HEALING

I am not a healer of long experience but I have attended courses with the National Federation of Spiritual Healers and have practised in a student capacity, so I would like to offer some observations on the practical possibilities of healing by contacting the Archangels. Many courses on healing suggest using colour vibrations and offer methods to open up the chakras; often healers will also make use of crystals. I mentioned earlier that I met one of the Archangels, Hanael, while I was doing some healing and that this enabled me identify its role in the healing process. Once this had happened I started to look for Archangels as I was working on the etheric body. I observed that the colour of the Archangels can be muddied or faded when they are not functioning at their full vibrational level in a particular soul/body complex. My approach to any Archangel which is obviously not blooming is to remind it of the appropriate task – this reminding is not a petition or a prayer but should be a command, stated with authority to provoke activity. The Archangels are part of our own invisible structure. We contain all these archetypes and their ability to assist in the process of re-balancing can only proceeed with our own inclination. The act of commanding creates a sense of purpose; it opens a dynamic channel – rather like the old magic formula 'Open Sesame'! The relationship with the Archangels is one in which all parties are obliged by divine law to work towards harmony and unification; it is not a privilege to speak with them but a natural and proper activity in which we should be constantly engaged.

No doubt the person who is being healed has obscure reasons for unconsciously overdeveloping a relationship with one Archangel or another, and the natal chart will supply some information that will help reveal these reasons. The astrological symbolism will allow the person to observe the underlying mechanism, to dust out his/her psychic corners and cleanse the inner lightbulbs so that all the Archetypes get a look in. As well as acknowledging that there may be very old causes, possibly in past lives, for the present dis-ease, the client can also be encouraged to envision her/his own body as a Tree and all the Archangels as power points.*
When I conduct a healing I work from the feet upward, calling on each Archangel as I move my hands upwards, hovering over the etheric body

---

* You will find exercises for meditation in the companion volume to this book, *Working with Angels*.

and stopping whenever I receive an inner visual clue to what is going on in the patient's soul/body complex. Sometimes I have found that an Archangel has almost no presence at all or has been overtaken by a demon which needs to be encouraged to transform itself. It is the case, obviously, that the seat occupied by each Archangel is continuously under threat from an opposite number, for every Archangel there is an Archdemon waiting in the wings! The one can slide into being the other very gradually, but when the balance has tipped too far in the other direction then some outward manifestation will make this obvious. In a man with a deep depression, hardly able to communicate, I found Samael looking like lead, a dark grey, sullen, immovable lump. Its delicate snowflake crystals had been transformed into chain mail. I am afraid to say the man did not return after the first consultation and I was unable to do any work to help him wake up the Angelic nature of the archetype.

The Archdemons are not opposing forces, but are neglected archetypes; they either hassle us to create a new, balanced life, by stirring up trouble, or they sink into an apathy, draining the life-force. We only have to pay due attention equally to the Archangels and everything becomes light and bright; the shadows are an illusion of our own making, the so-called 'dark forces' represent the natural tendencies we have to entropy – when we forget to polish our front door knob the grey sludge can soon take over. Working with Archangels is about keeping our archetypes polished; it is about keeping the windows of our inner world clean and sparkling.

Whenever I begin healing I call on Raphael to watch over and guide me, as well as to energize the patient's own resources. Then I work methodically over the body and speak to the Archangels on the inner level, explaining what I see to be the problem and asking them to shift into more harmonious dynamic: the reason for disharmony is a direct consequence of the patient's mind-set and is not the fault of an Archangel! The healer's task is to gently over-ride the psychic malfunctioning and remind the underlying structure of its proper function – just as a chiropractor or osteopath will manipulate at the skeletal level, encouraging a return to the natural and original intention of the organism, so the healer manipulates at a psychic level, reminding the patient's metaphysical system of its own real need and desire, which is to be a creature living to the full potential of mind, body, spirit, and emotion.

There are many healers who use crystals and they have some obvious links with the Archangels. The two most widely used crystals are rose quartz and amethyst and I feel these two draw on Zaphkiel and Raphael respectively, and there are bound to be crystals which connect with the other Archangels. One of my main reasons for not using crystals myself is that there is no real need to use them – we can call on our own inner resources to make contact, through the bridging agency of the Archangels, with the metaphysical structures which promote healing. Whereas crystals may be useful tools, it would be helpful to develop beyond the necessity for their use, if only to save Mother Earth from further desecration.

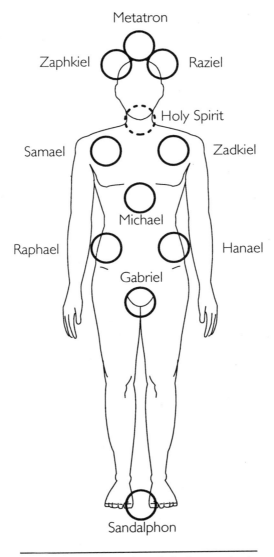

Figure 7   Archangels and the human body

APPENDIX FOUR

ARCHANGELS AND MANIFESTATION

The process by which the invisible makes itself manifest is very clearly defined in the Tree of Life by the lightning flash, the descent from Crown to Kingdom and it is obvious that all the Archangels are involved in this unfolding. If we wish to participate in this creativity at the deepest level we need firstly to recognize the role which is played by all the archetypes and to consciously attune to them. A more direct and more powerful involvement is possible if we can achieve a state of quietness which allows us to commune with the Divine at the top of the Tree and converse with the three supernal Archangels. This state is achieved during the practise of transcendental meditation and some students learn advanced techniques, called siddhis, which are based on the Yoga Sutras or *Aphorisms of Yoga* of Patanjali, which probably date back about 2,000 years The practitioner settles her/himself into a deep state of meditation and introduces a very simple thought, based on a desire to create and manifest something in the real world. This technique is used to produce some unusual effects – such as levitation – and Bede Griffiths, a Benedictine monk who lived, until his recent death, in an ashram, has suggested that Jesus was using siddhi techniques when he walked on water and performed other miracles. A person in an expanded state of consciousness has an uncontrived relationship with the creative powers of the universe and becomes a natural miracle worker and healer. Lesser mortals will have to be more self-conscious and perform regular exercises in dipping into this well of unbounded creativity, just as a musician has to practise regular scales before she/he builds up an effortless and intimate relationship with the instrument.

We can develop techniques based on a model like the Tree of Life, or the Spiritual Alphabet used by sixteenth century mystics, like Teresa of Avila and John of the Cross, or on the Sufi Manual *Journey to the Lord of Power*, or on the transcendental meditation of Maharishi: all of them are directed at the same goal. The Tree of Life has a very precise structure which can be 'climbed'; then we can stand before the throne of Metatron and make our intentions known: 'this is what I want to create and I believe it is for the good, not only my personal good but good for those around me'. In order to draw power from this source we do need to be as free as possible from selfish and greedy motives. This is not to say that the power will not switch on if there are questionable motives, it certainly does, as numerous examples in the political and business world will demonstrate, but the results will eventually be negative and the projects will collapse in on themselves because all the archetypes will not be satisfied and the Tree will not be balanced. It is as though a plant had a root system which only nourished part of the plant — the part which is starved will die and the whole plant will suffer. Robert Maxwell's empire had immense power but it was based almost entirely on energy from the right hand side of the tree, as is often the case in business and politics. He called too loudly on Hanael and Zadkiel and forgot to balance their power with that of Raphael and Samael. This lack of balance leads to dysfunction; this applies to organizations, living organisms, patterns of consciousness, the whole planet. The Nazi regime suffered the same kind of fate – it seems likely that Hitler was quite consciously tuned in to methods of manifesting his desires, since he actually used a lightning flash as one of his symbols, but he was pathologically unable to tune in to the energy of Raphael or Michael; had he done so he might have helped to facilitate a Golden Age rather than an Iron Regime. The whole mood of a personality who functions in a balanced relationship to the archetypes will prevent her/him becoming a dictator as she/he would see themselves as part of a whole, serving by leading.

AFTERWORD

I would like to close this book with a small tribute to John Blackwood who was born in Edinburgh on 27th January 1943 and lived in Oxford for many years until his death on 24th April 1993.

John was an author, piano teacher, tutor, and editor, with a keen interest in philosophy, cosmology and music. He was an active member of the Oxford Astrology Group and also a poet: his first book, a collection of poems, *The Early Education of a Deep Sea Diver*, was puublished in 1970. He wrote books on diverse subjects such as *Oxford's Gargoyles and Grotesques* (highly recommended if you visit Oxford) and *Garlic – Nature's Original Remedy*. His early death is a keen loss to those who knew him.

The Early Education of a Deep Sea Diver demonstrates John's acute awareness of myth and a deep understanding of the great archetypes. I would like to thank him for the editing work he did on this book and the encouragement he gave me with presenting its contents to a wider audience. The following extract from his poem *Spring Myth* is an entirely appropriate note on which to close:

And we said,
'We are not to be found anywhere.
We crouch in the needle's eye,
In the cowslip's bell
Poised upon the golden pollen rod.
And we have seen what is going on,
And, as before, we give it our blessing.

We watch
And from chaos worlds freely arise
According to a form and pattern
Ordained from before time.

We are the myth makers, the tellers of the tale;
We are the chroniclers of our own event.
Our science is unending accuracy.
We watch.

We are the horn that runs you through
To be the middle of the brow;
We died upon the cross for you,
And live again as here is now.

Our tongues are the roots of trees, are lark's tongues,
and our Leviathan's a merry tune in the sea's belly.

These are our songs; you may sing of them
whatsoever songs please you.'

INDEX

117

CAER SIDI

Centre for Advanced Education,

Research and Studies in Divine Intelligence

This is the first book to be published by CAER SIDI, Centre for Advanced Education, Research and Studies in Divine Intelligence. The Centre was set up in 1994 by Theolyn Cortens and her husband, Will Shaman, in order to ease the transitions that we will be facing in our changing world. The Centre's aim is to help individuals realize how powerful they are and to facilitate education and experience in life-supporting activities that embrace a wide variety of fields, including the arts, metaphysics, practical skills, and to encourage a sense of the sacred. These activities are essentially life-enhancing in their own right, as well as necessary for the recreation of a sustainable way of life for the future, and we hope our efforts will act as a catalyst for others to set up similar groups themselves as we claim no exclusive right to handling the future!

Our logo is based on a six pointed star which, as Judaism recognizes, represents the union of Heaven and Earth. CAER SIDI is committed to fostering this union in any way possible, and to this end seeks to construct a six-sided building for its activities, designed and sited on geomantic principles. Further details of this project will be published separately.

Membership of CAER SIDI is invited for a modest fee. Members are entitled to a generous discount on a wide variety of workshops and talks, as well as a quarterly newsletter, *The Star*. In addition, ceremonial festivities are held eight times a year to which all members are welcome. For further details and a copy of the CAER SIDI manifesto, *A proposition for a new establishment*, please send a large sae to the address below.

JOIN THE CAER SIDI MAILING LIST

Write to us at the address below and we will keep you informed of new books, audio-tapes, workshops and courses on Angels and Sacred Sound Meditation.

CAER SIDI, Hencroft, Main Road, Long Hanborough, Oxon OX8 8LA